MOVIE VOCAL SELECTIONS

ISBN 978-1-4234-0626-6

HAL•LEONARD®
CORPORATION
7777 W. BLUEMOUND RD. P.O. BOX 13819 MILWAUKEE, WI 53213

In Australia Contact:
Hal Leonard Australia Pty. Ltd.
4 Lentara Court
Cheltenham, Victoria, 3192 Australia
Email: ausadmin@halleonard.com

Visit Hal Leonard Online at
www.halleonard.com

SEASONS OF LOVE

Words and Music by
JONATHAN LARSON

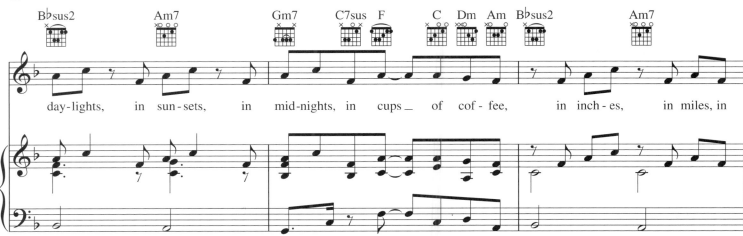

day-lights, in sun-sets, in mid-nights, in cups __ of cof-fee, in inch-es, in miles, in

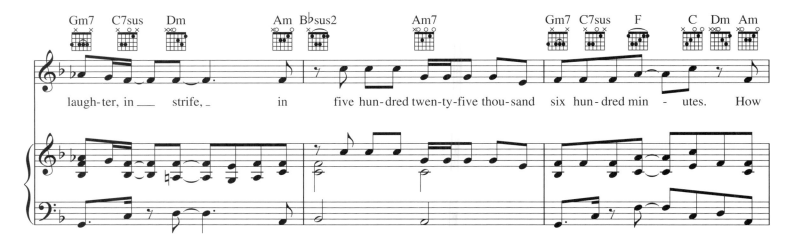

laugh-ter, in ___ strife, _ in five hun-dred twen-ty-five thou-sand six hun-dred min - utes. How

do you meas-ure a year in ___ the life? _ How a-bout love? _____

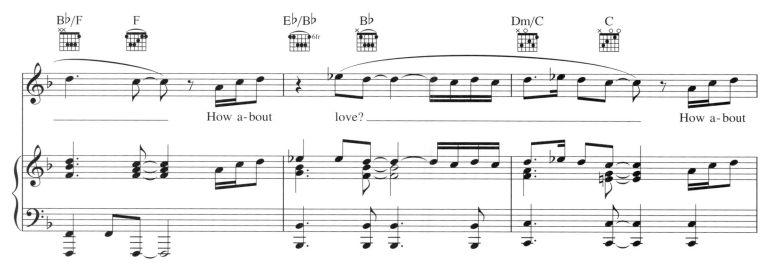

_____ How a-bout love? _____ How a-bout

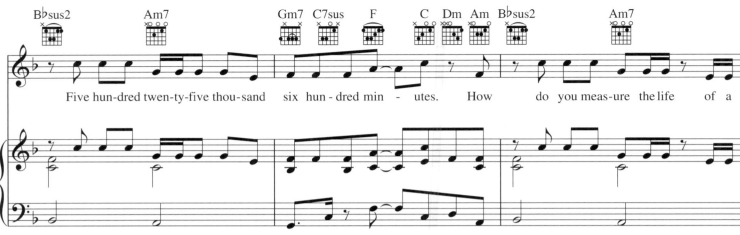

Five hun-dred twen-ty-five thou-sand six hun-dred min - utes. How do you meas-ure the life of a

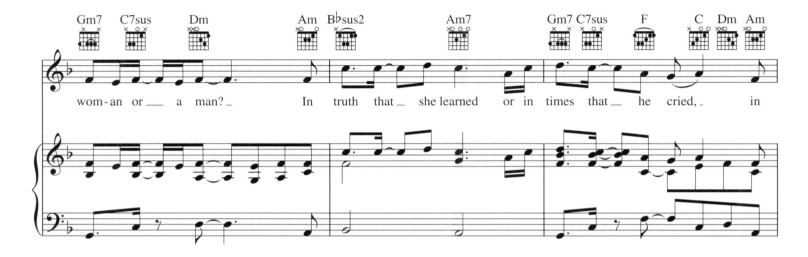

wom-an or ___ a man? _ In truth that _ she learned or in times that _ he cried, _ in

bridg-es ___ he burned or the way that she died. _____ It's time now to sing out, though the

sto-ry nev - er ends. ___ Let's cel - e - brate, re-mem - ber a year in the life of ___ friends. _ Re-mem-ber the

RENT

Words and Music by
JONATHAN LARSON

Bright Rock

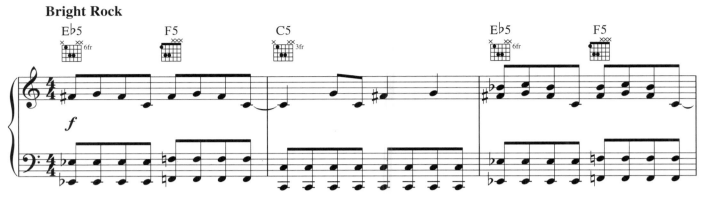

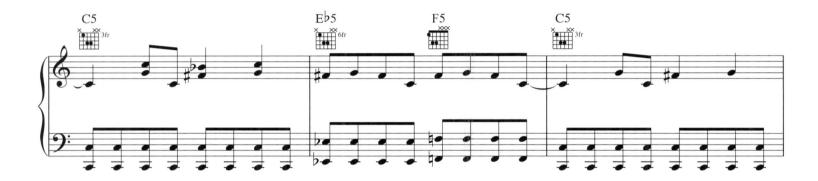

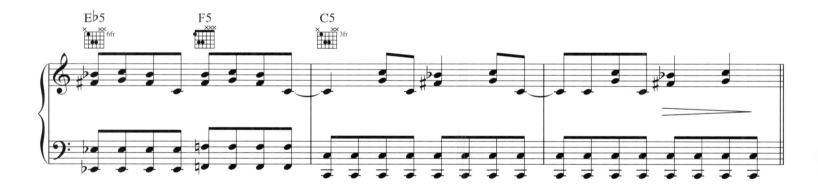

How do you doc - u - ment _ real life when real life's

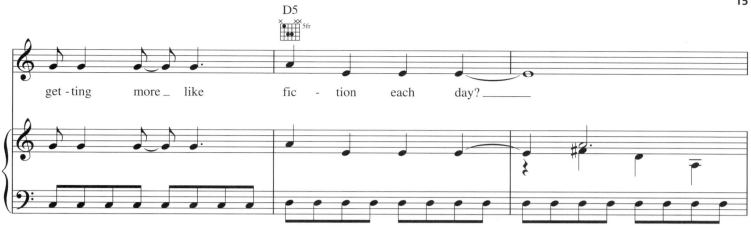

get-ting more _ like fic - tion each day? _____

Head - lines, bread lines blow my mind, _ and now ___ this dead - line; e -

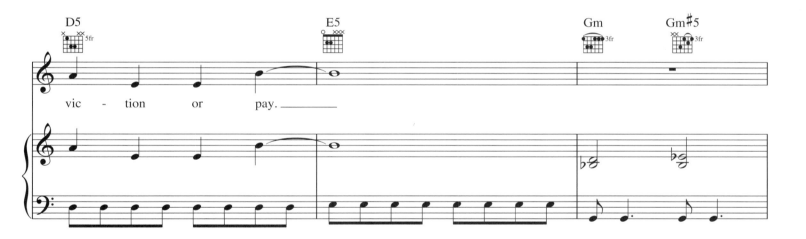

vic - tion or pay. _____

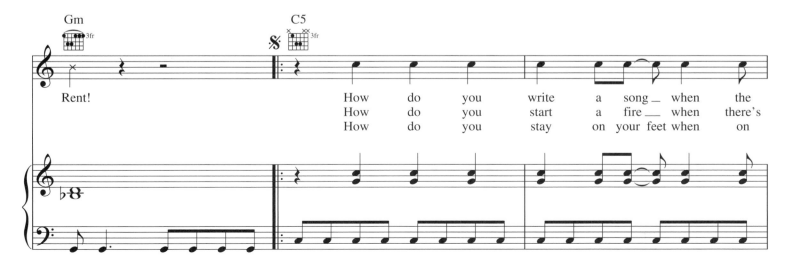

Rent!

How do you write a song _ when the
How do you start a fire _ when there's
How do you stay on your feet when on

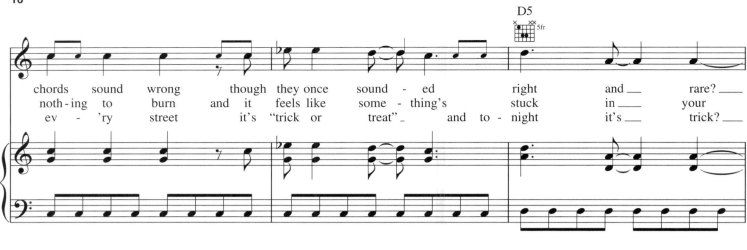

chords sound wrong though they once sound - ed right and __ rare? __
noth - ing to burn and it feels like some - thing's stuck in __ your
ev - 'ry street it's "trick or treat" _ and to - night it's __ trick? __

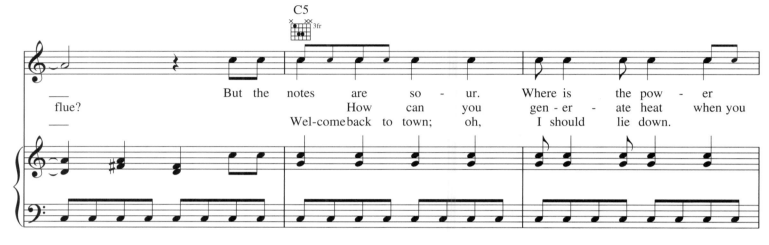

__ flue?
But the notes are so - ur. Where is the pow - er
Wel - come back to town; oh, I should lie down.

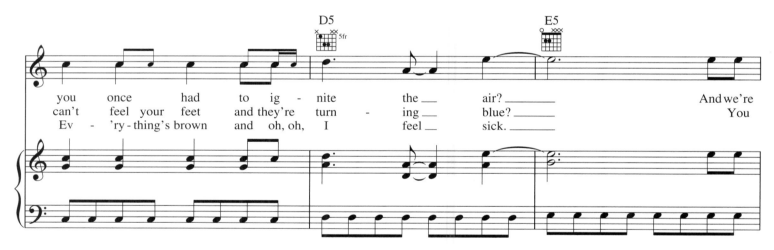

you once had to ig - nite the __ air? _____
can't feel your feet and they're turn - ing __ blue? _____
Ev - 'ry - thing's brown and oh, oh, I feel __ sick. _____

And we're
You

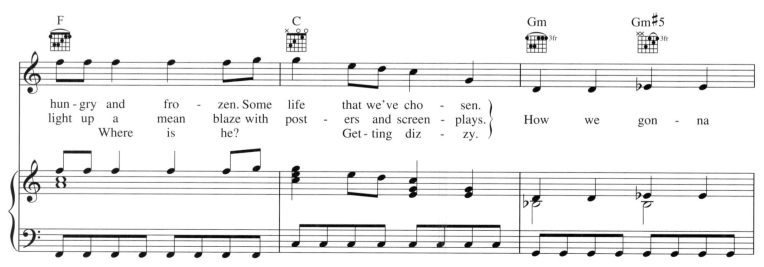

hun - gry and fro - zen. Some life that we've cho - sen.
light up a mean blaze with post - ers and screen - plays.
Where is he? Get - ting diz - zy.

How we gon - na

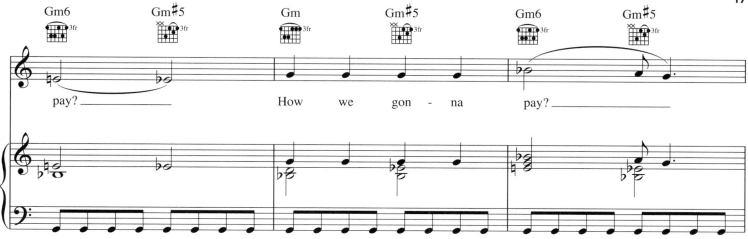

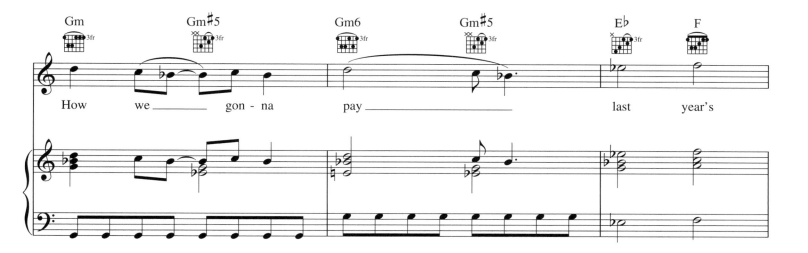

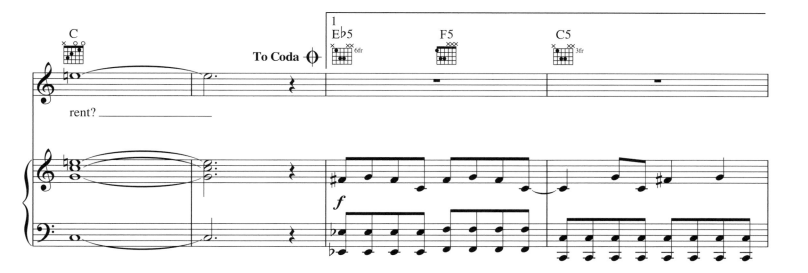

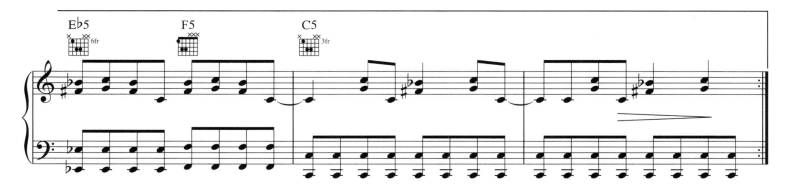

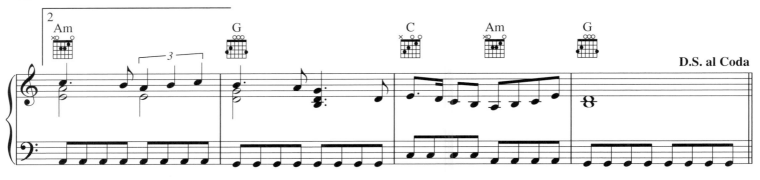

D.S. al Coda

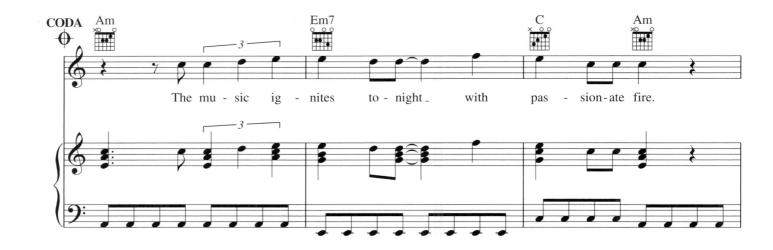

CODA

The mu - sic ig - nites to - night _ with pas - sion - ate fire.

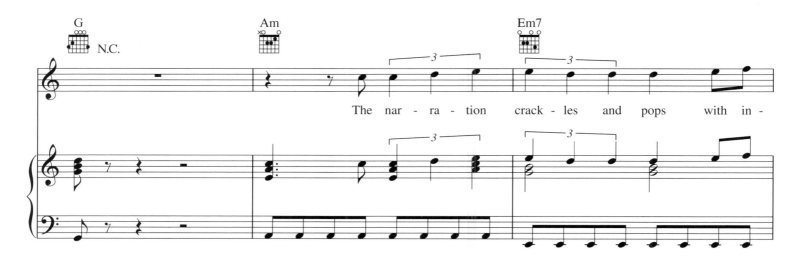

The nar - ra - tion crack - les and pops with in -

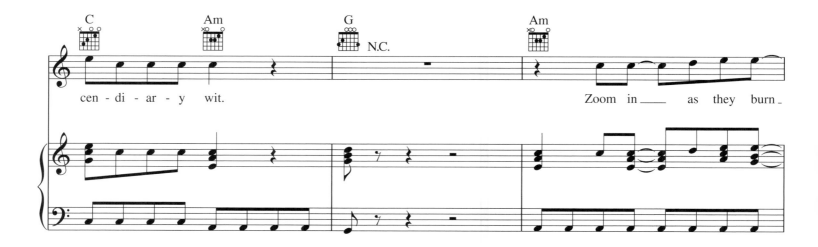

cen - di - ar - y wit.

Zoom in ___ as they burn _

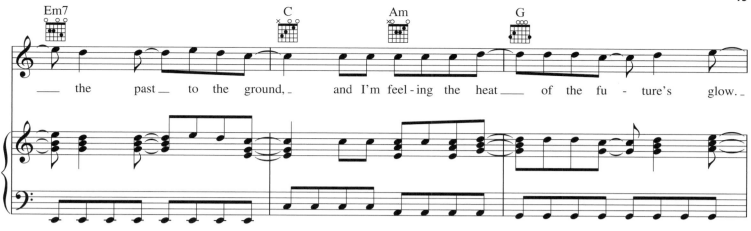

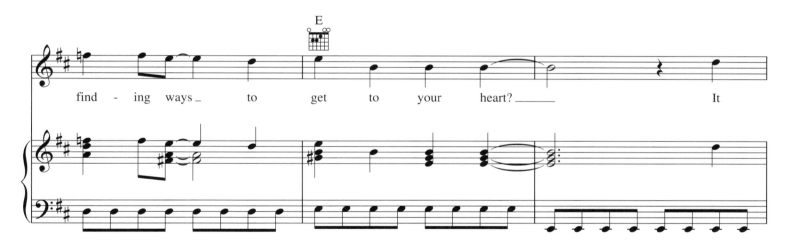

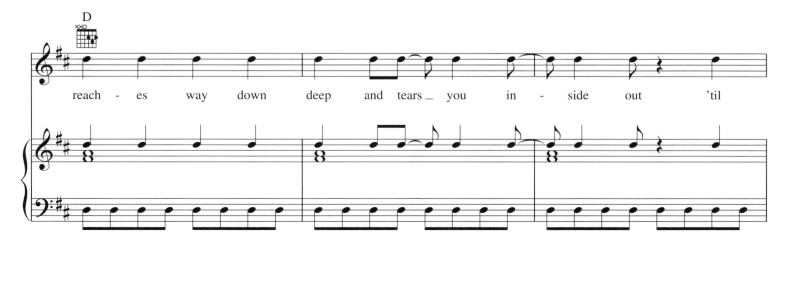

you're torn __ a - part. __ Rent! How can __ you con-

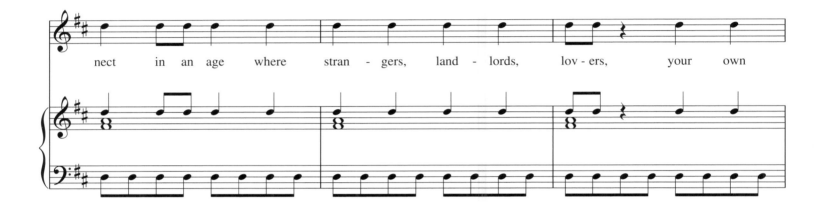

nect in an age where stran - gers, land - lords, lov - ers, your own

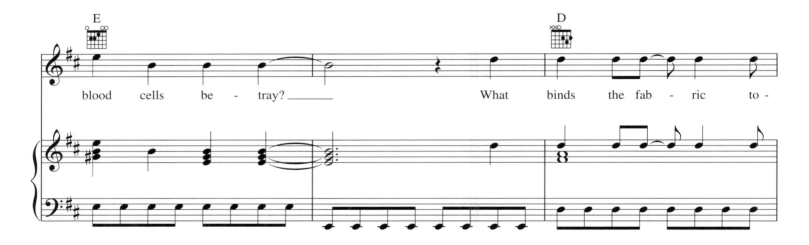

blood cells be - tray? _____ What binds the fab - ric to -

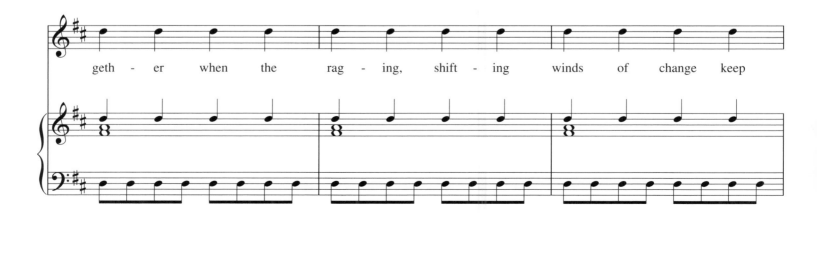

geth - er when the rag - ing, shift - ing winds of change keep

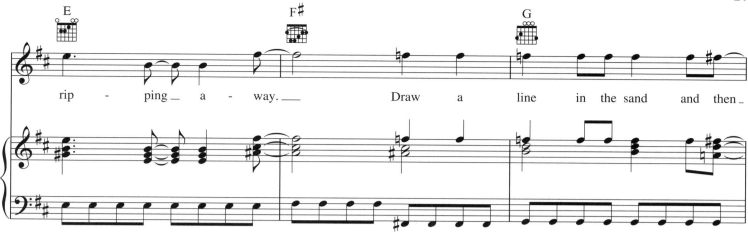

rip - ping _ a - way. ___ Draw a line in the sand and then _

___ make a stand. Use your cam - era to spar, _ use ___ your gui - tar. When

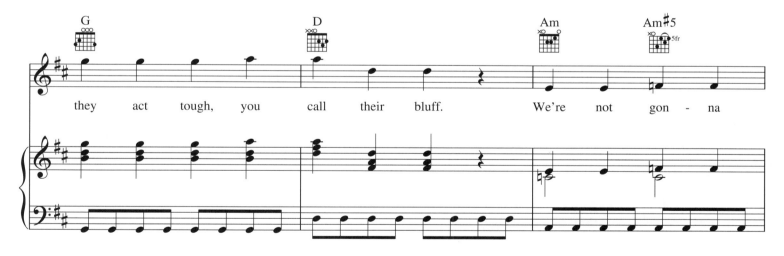

they act tough, you call their bluff. We're not gon - na

pay. _____ We're not gon - na pay. _____

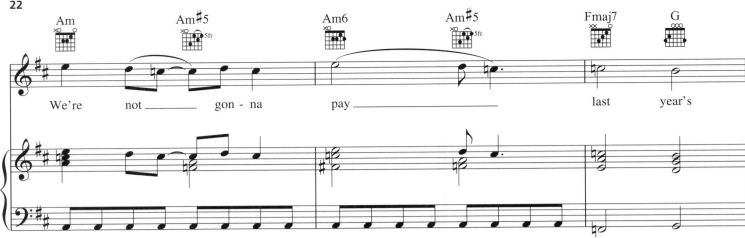

We're not _____ gon - na pay _____ last year's

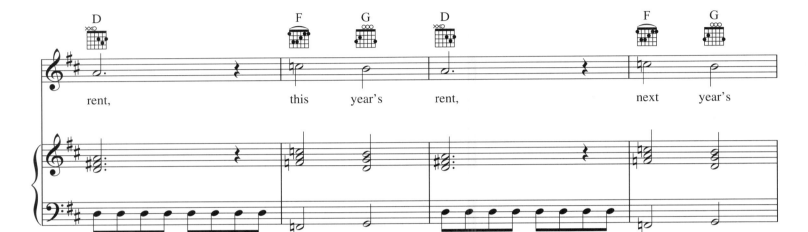

rent, this year's rent, next year's

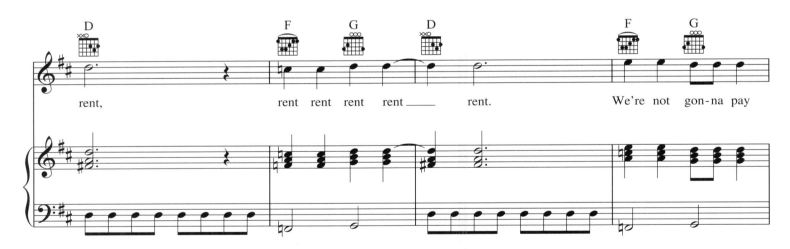

rent, rent rent rent rent ____ rent. We're not gon-na pay

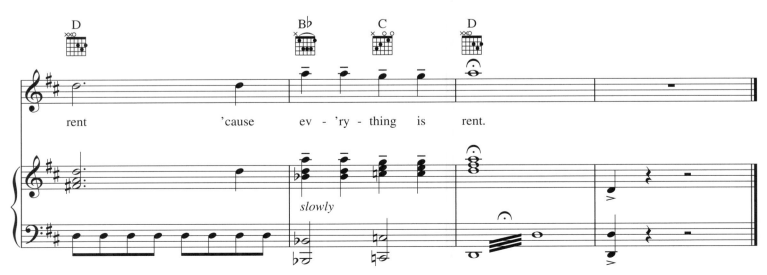

rent 'cause ev - 'ry - thing is rent.

slowly

YOU'LL SEE

Words and Music by
JONATHAN LARSON

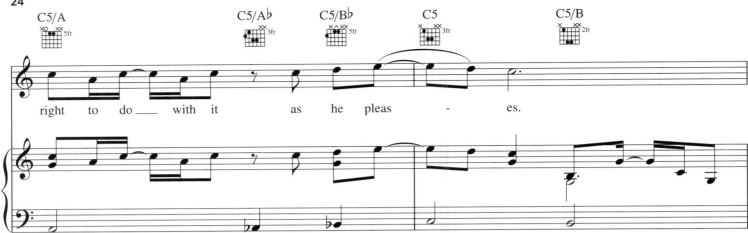

right to do ___ with it as he pleas - es.

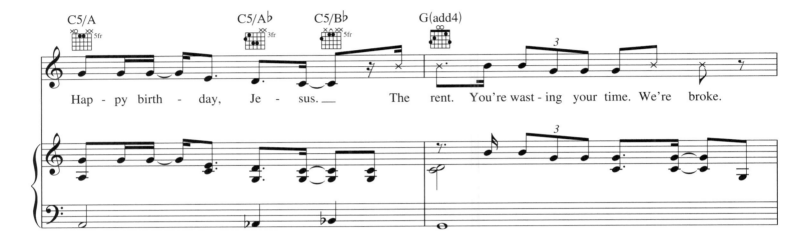

Hap - py birth - day, Je - sus. ___ The rent. You're wast - ing your time. We're broke.

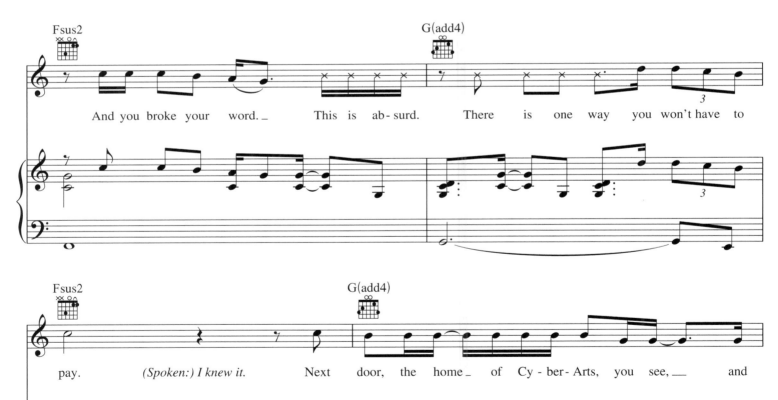

And you broke your word. _ This is ab - surd. There is one way you won't have to

pay. *(Spoken:) I knew it.* Next door, the home _ of Cy - ber - Arts, you see, ___ and

now that the block is re- zoned, ___ our dream can __ be - come ___ a re-

al - i - ty. ___ You'll see, ___ boys. _____ You'll see, _

___ boys. _____ *(Spoken:) A state-of-the-art, digital, virtual, interactive studio.*

I'll for - go your rent, ___ and on

pa - per guar - an - tee ___ that you can stay here ___ for free. ___

(Spoken:) If you do me one small favor. What? Convince Maureen to cancel her protest. Why not just get an

injection or call the cops? Yeah, I did, and they're on standby. But my in -

vest - ors ___ would rath - er ___ I han - dle this qui - et - ly.

ONE SONG GLORY

from RENT

Words and Music by
JONATHAN LARSON

Moderately

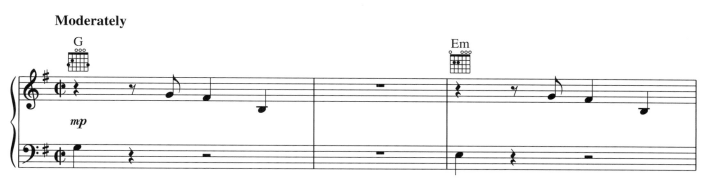

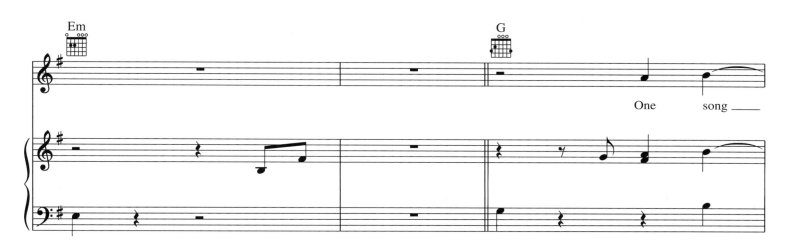

One song _____

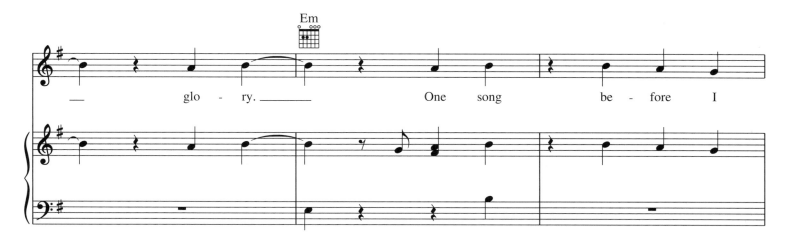

_____ glo - ry. _____ One song be - fore I

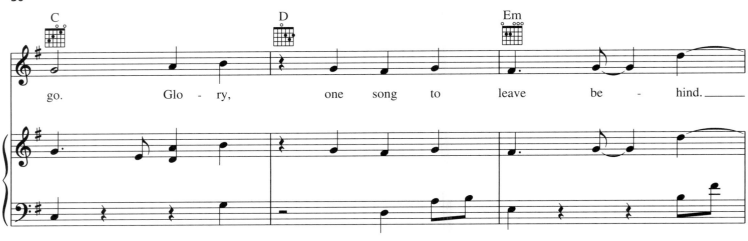

go. Glo - ry, one song to leave be - hind. _____

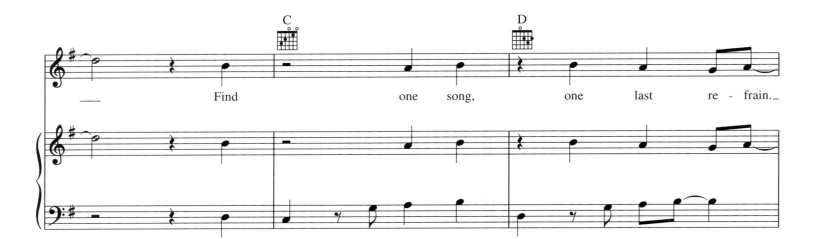

_____ Find one song, one last re - frain. _____

_____ Glo - ry _____ from the pret - ty boy front man _____

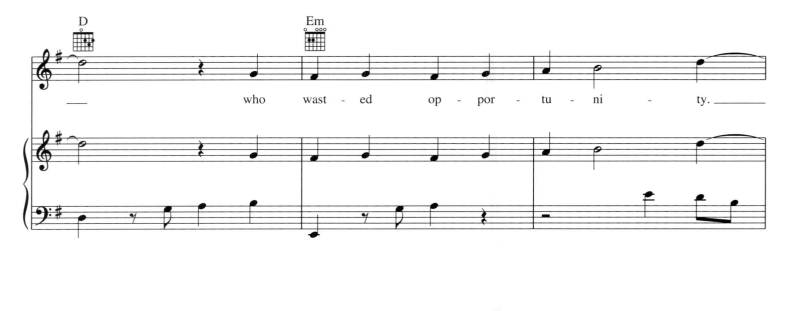

_____ who wast - ed op - por - tu - ni - ty. _____

One song, _____ he had the world at his feet. Glo - ry _____

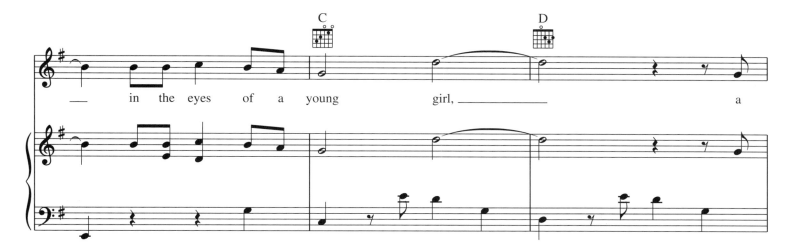

_____ in the eyes of a young girl, _____ a

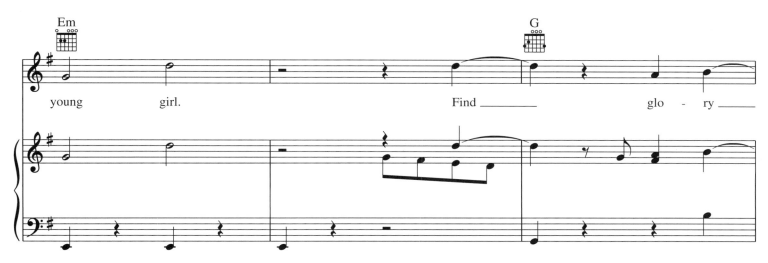

young girl. Find _____ glo - ry _____

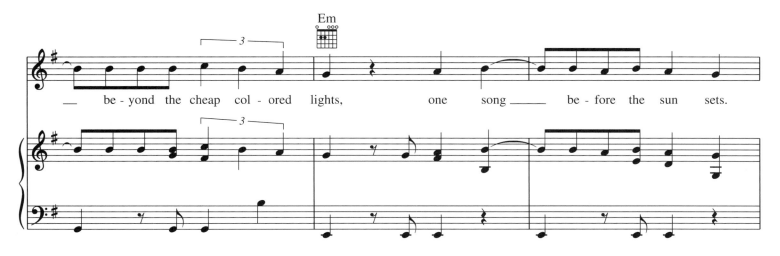

_____ be - yond the cheap col - ored lights, one song _____ be - fore the sun sets.

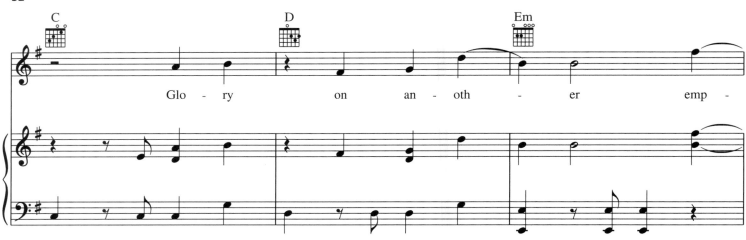

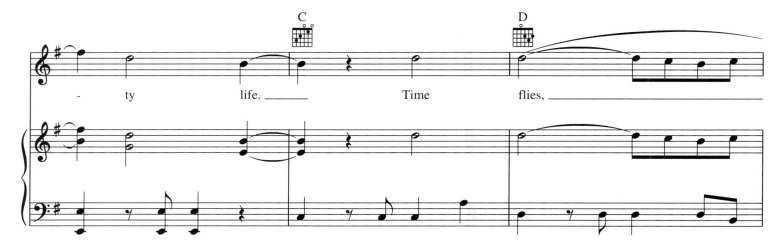

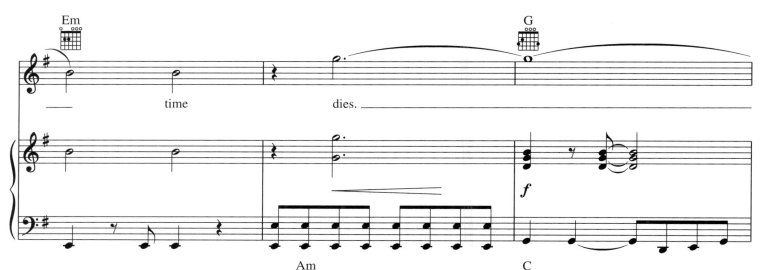

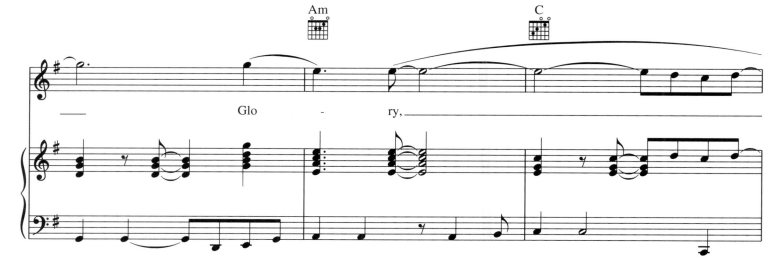

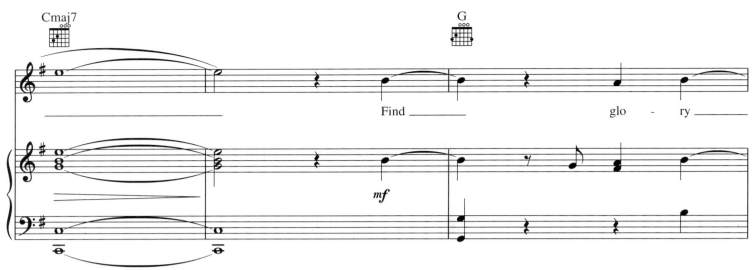

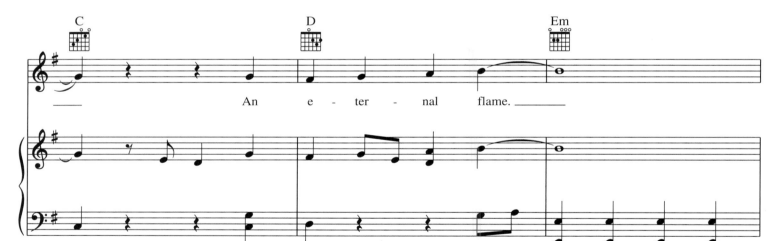

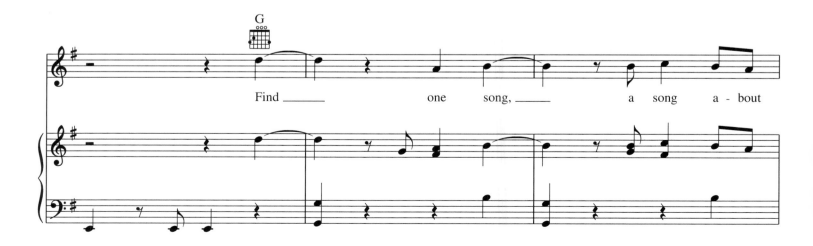

love. Glo - ry _____ from the soul of a young man, _____

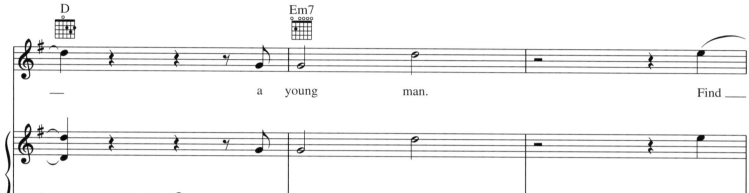

— a young man. Find ___

the one song be - fore the vi - rus takes hold, glo - ry

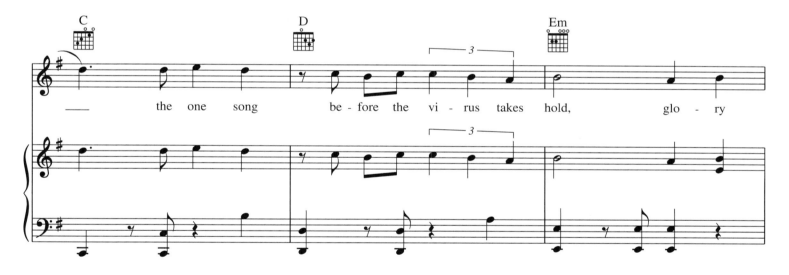

like a sun - set. One song to re - deem___

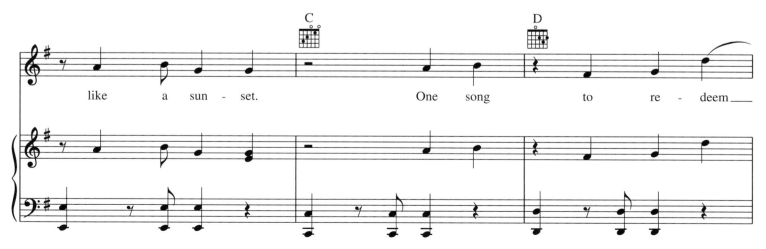

LIGHT MY CANDLE

Words and Music by
JONATHAN LARSON

And I'm just a lit - tle weak on my ____ feet.
Sor - ry 'bout your friend.

Would you light my ____ can - dle? _____

What are you star - ing at? Noth - ing. __ Your hair in the moon -

light. _____ You look fa - mil - iar.

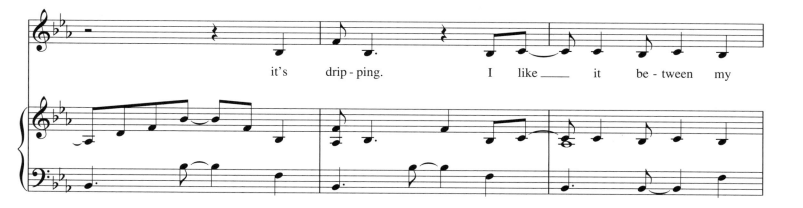

fin - gers.   I fig - ured.   Oh, well,   good - night.

(Drum break)

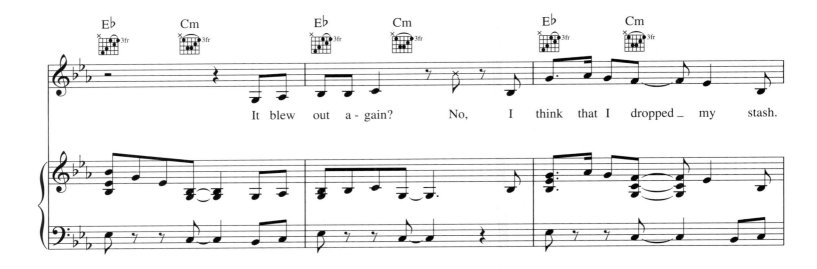

It blew out a - gain?   No,   I think that I dropped _ my   stash.

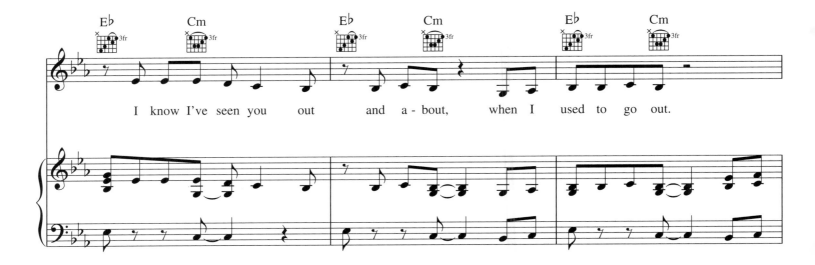

I know I've seen you   out   and a - bout,   when I   used to go out.

Your can-dle's out. I'm ill-in', I had it when I walked in the door.

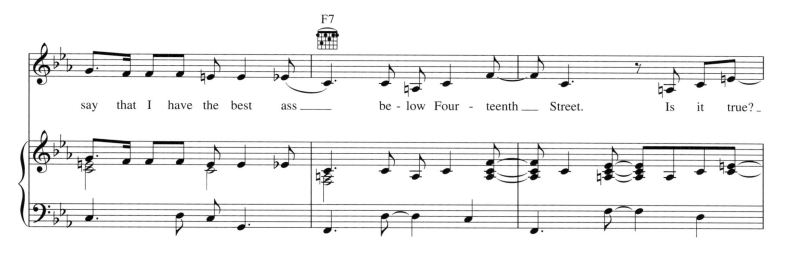

It was pure. Is it on the floor? *(Spoken:) The floor?* They

say that I have the best ass _____ be-low Four-teenth _____ Street. Is it true? _

_ What? You're star-in' a-gain. _ Oh, no. I mean, you do.

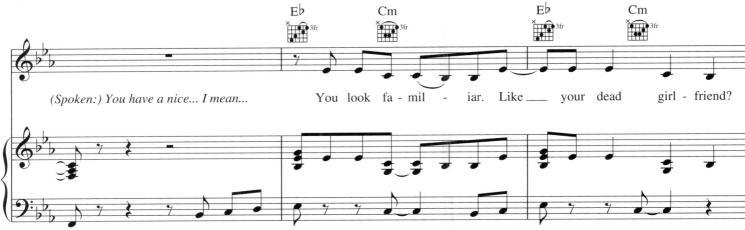

(Spoken:) *You have a nice... I mean...* You look fa - mil - iar. Like ___ your dead girl - friend?

On - ly when you smile, but I'm sure I've seen ___ you some - where

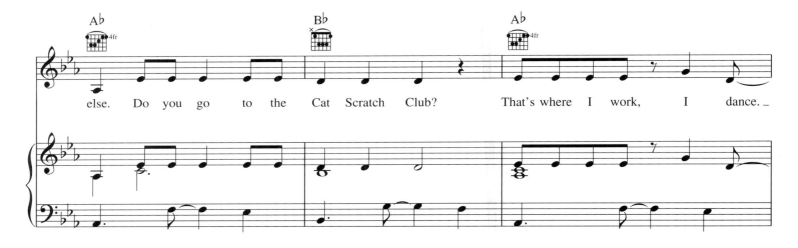

else. Do you go to the Cat Scratch Club? That's where I work, I dance. ___

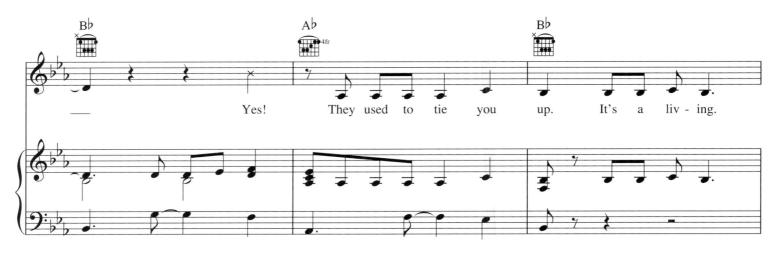

___ Yes! They used to tie you up. It's a liv - ing.

I did-n't rec-og-nize you with-out the hand-cuffs. We could _ light the _

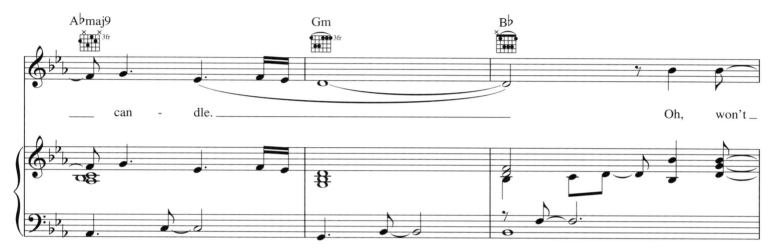

_ can - dle. _____ Oh, won't _

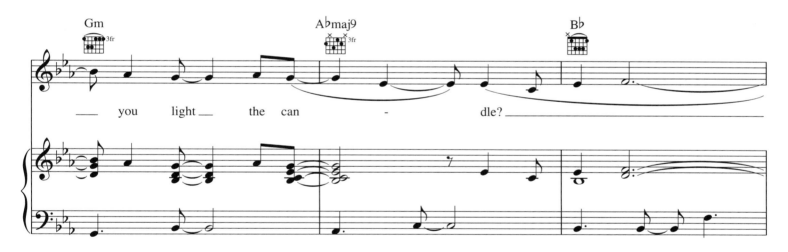

_ you light _ the can - dle? _____

Why don't _ you for-get that stuff? You look _

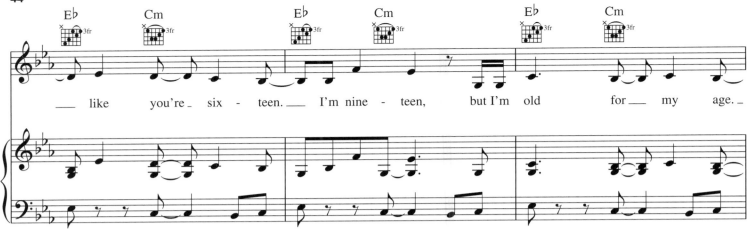

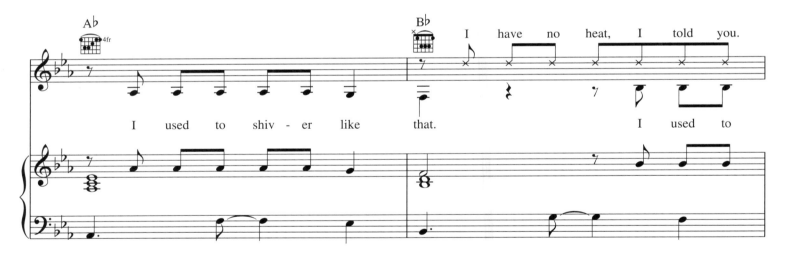

junk - ie. Now and then I like to feel good. *(Spoken:) Oh, here. What's that?*

Oh. Candy bar wrapper. We could light the can - dle.

Oh, what'd you do with my

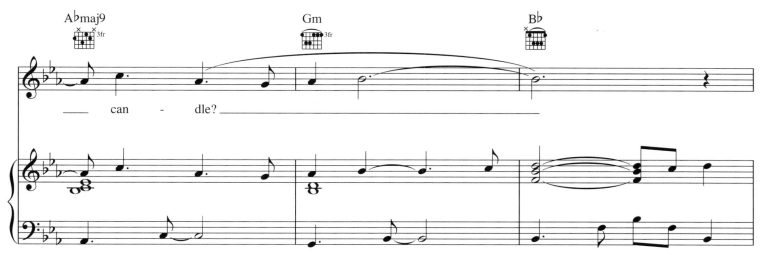

can - dle?

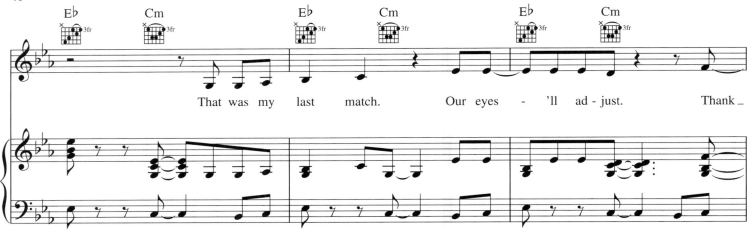

That was my last match. Our eyes - 'll ad - just. Thank _

_ God for _ the moon. May - be it's not _ the moon at all. I hear

Spike Lee's shoot - in' down the street. Bah, hum - bug.

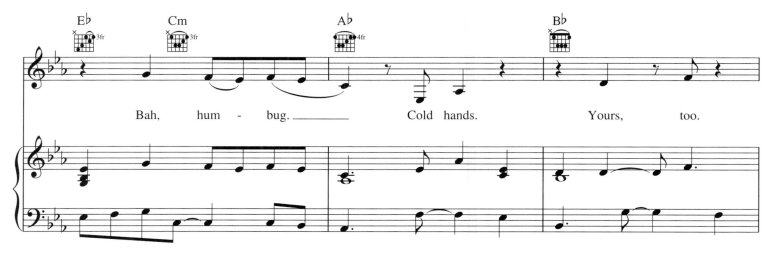

Bah, hum - bug. _____ Cold hands. Yours, too.

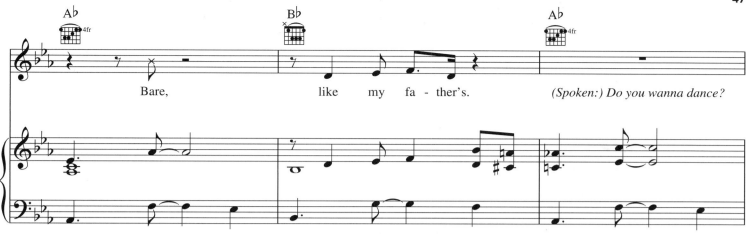

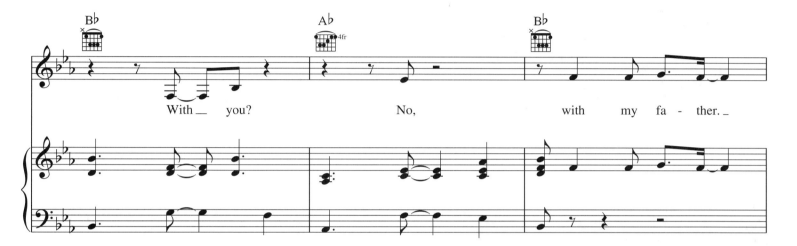

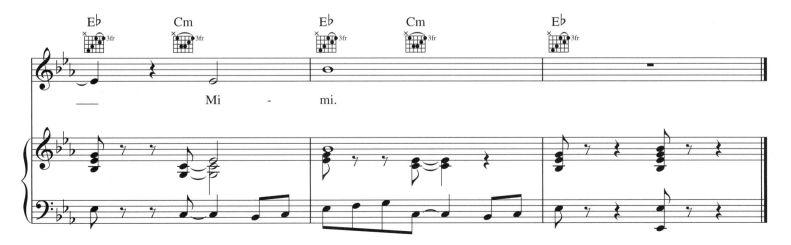

TANGO: MAUREEN

Words and Music by
JONATHAN LARSON

think-ing of drink-ing gas-o-line? *Female:* As a mat-ter of fact... Hon-ey,

I know this act, it's called the Tan-go Mau-reen. The

Tan-go Mau - reen, _____ it's a dark, diz-zy mer-ry-go-

round. As she keeps you dan-gling, _____ your

Female: You're wrong.

heart she is man - gling._____ And you toss and you turn, 'cause her
It's dif - f'rent with me.

cold eyes can burn, yet you yearn, and you churn, and re - bound. *Female:* I think I

know what you mean. *Both:* The Tan - go Mau - reen._____

Male: Has she ev - er pout - ed her lips and called you

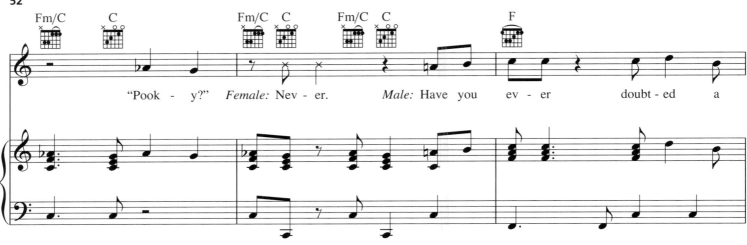

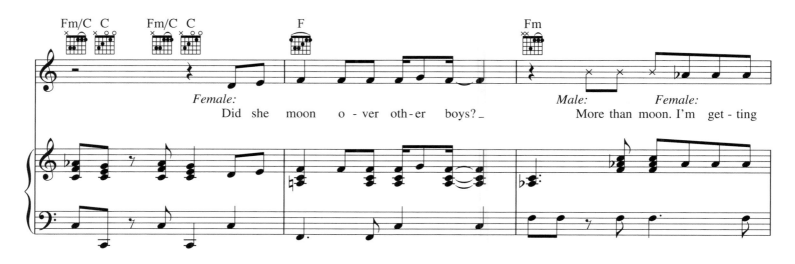

Play 4 times

nau - seous.

4th time only:

(Male:) Where'd you learn to tango?   (Female:) With the French ambassador's daughter, in her dorm room at Miss Porter's.

And you?   (Male:) With Nanette Himmelfarb,
the rabbi's daughter at the
Scarsdale Jewish Community Center.

It's hard to do this backwards.

Female: You should try it   in heels.

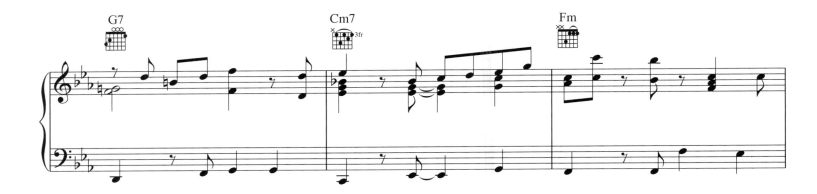

Female: *Male:* *Female:* *Male:* *Female:*
She cheat-ed. She cheat-ed. Mau-reen cheat-ed. Fuck-in' cheat-ed. I'm de-

glum, and you bum and turn blue. *Male:* Why do we love when she's mean? _____

Female: And she can be so ob - scene, _____

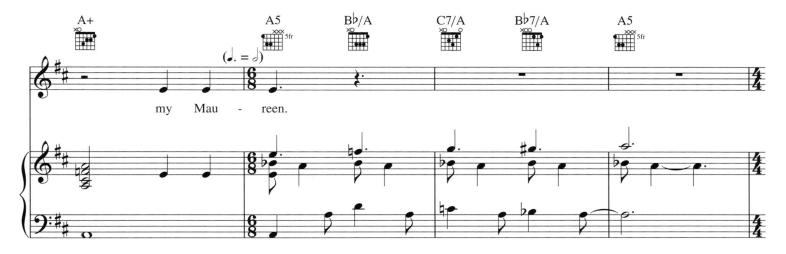

my Mau - reen.

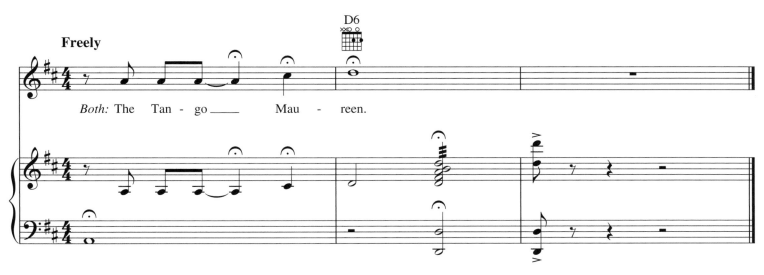

Both: The Tan - go _____ Mau - reen.

OUT TONIGHT

Words and Music by
JONATHAN LARSON

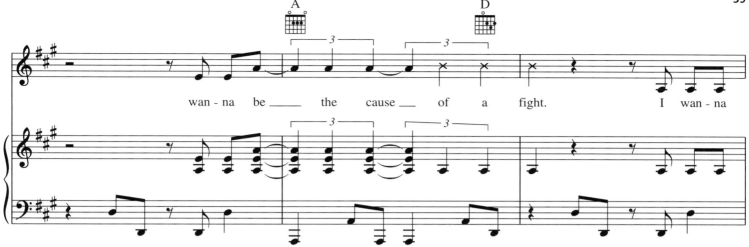

wan - na be ____ the cause ____ of a fight. I wan - na

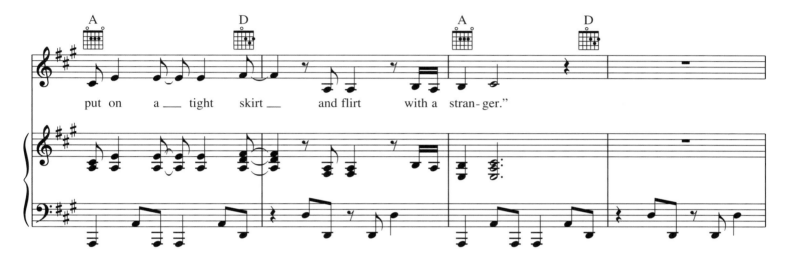

put on a ____ tight skirt ____ and flirt with a stran - ger."

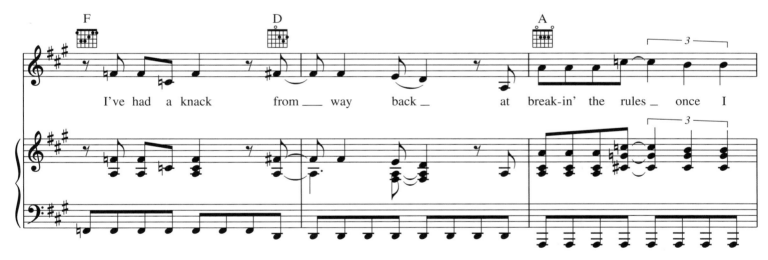

I've had a knack from ____ way back ____ at break-in' the rules ____ once I

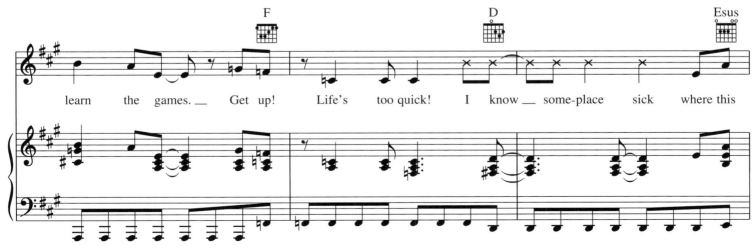

learn the games. ____ Get up! Life's too quick! I know ____ some-place sick where this

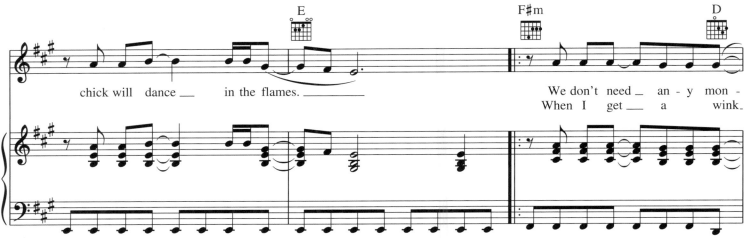

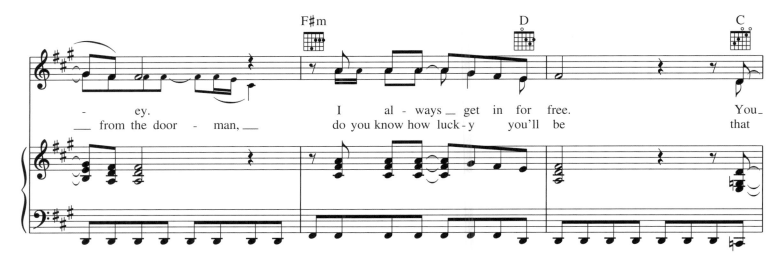

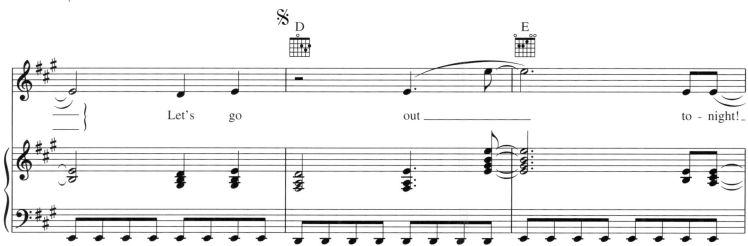

home when the Span-ish ba-bies cry. _____ So let's find a

bar _____ so dark we for-get who we are, and all the scars of the

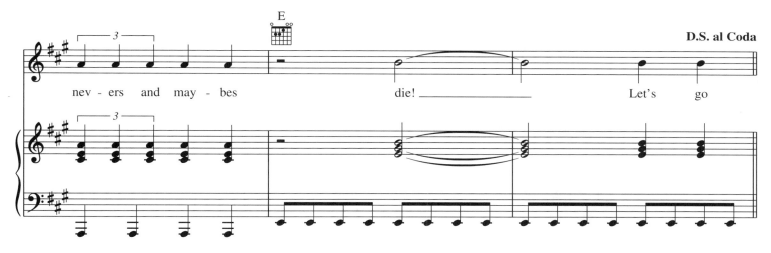

D.S. al Coda

nev-ers and may-bes die! _____ Let's go

CODA

You're sweet, wan-na hit the street, _ wan-na wail at the moon _ like a cat _

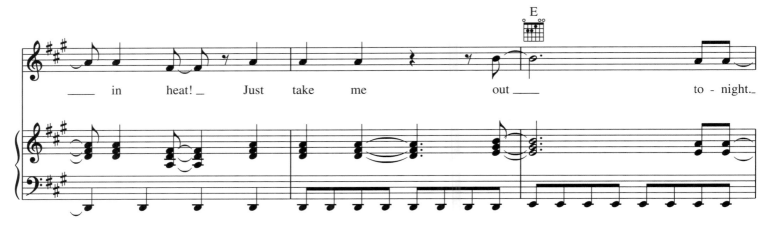

in heat! __ Just take me out __ to-night..

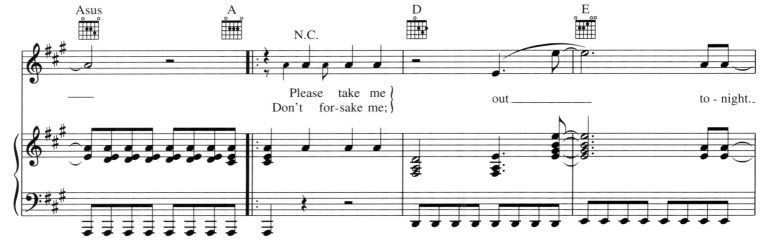

Please take me
Don't for-sake me; } out __ to-night..

I'll let you make me! __ Out __ to-night,_

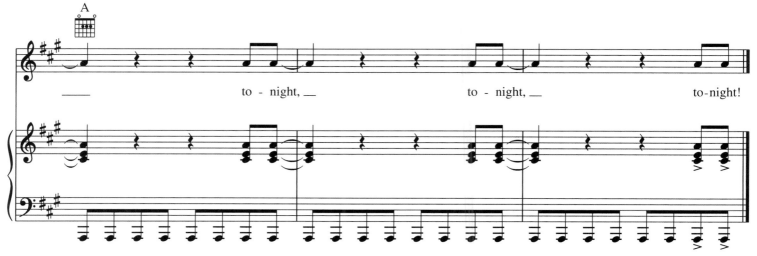

to-night, __ to-night, __ to-night!

ANOTHER DAY

Words and Music by
JONATHAN LARSON

Take your pow-der, take your can - dle. Your sweet whis-per I

just can't han - dle. Well, take ___ your hair ___ in the moon - light,

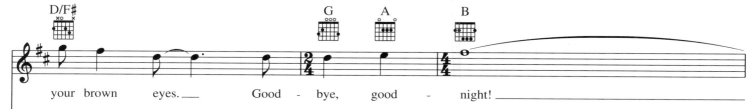

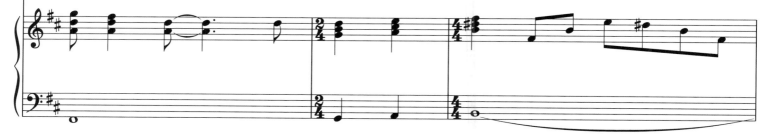

your brown eyes. ___ Good - bye, good - night! _____

___ I should tell ___ you, I should tell ___ you.

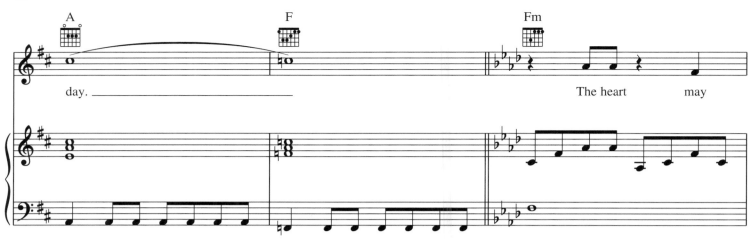

day. _____ The heart may

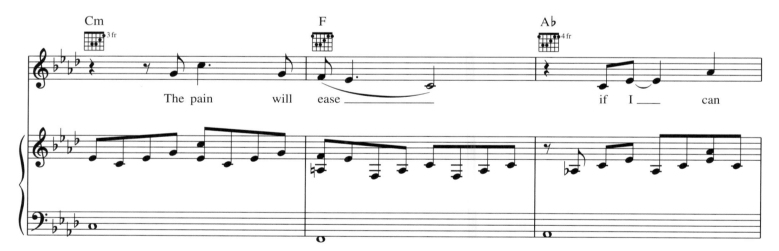

freeze, _____ or it can burn. _____

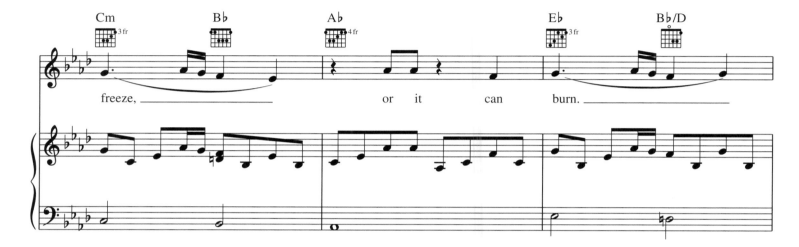

The pain will ease _____ if I ____ can

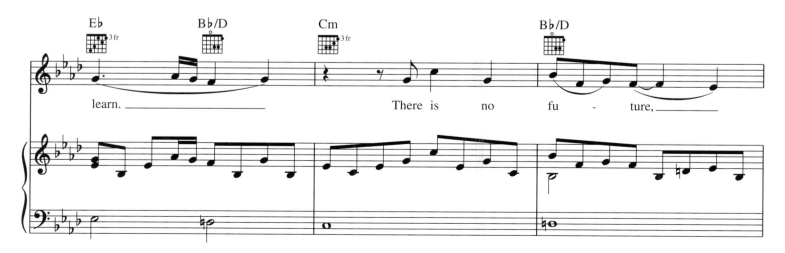

learn. _____ There is no fu - ture, _____

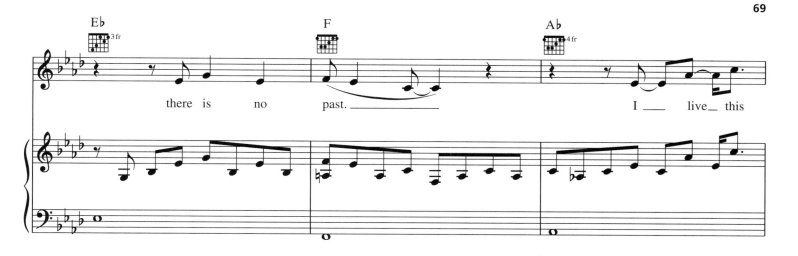

there is no past. _____ I ___ live ___ this

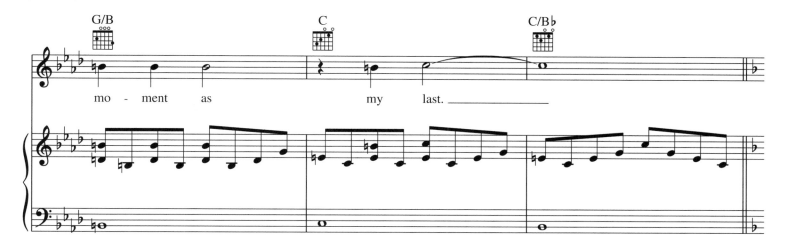

mo - ment as my last. _____

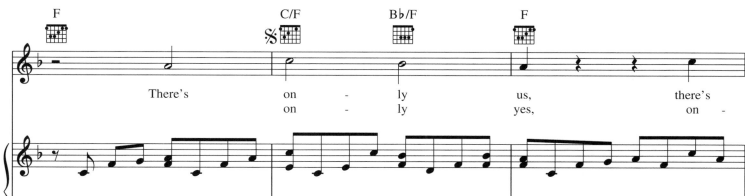

There's on - ly us, there's
on - ly yes,   on -

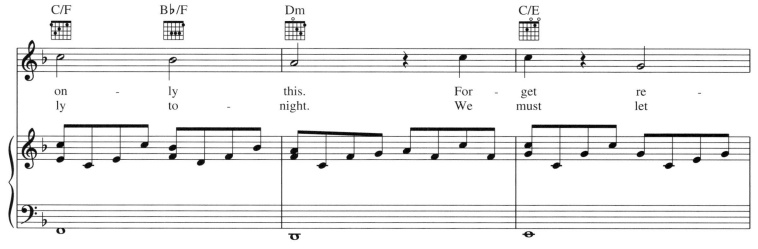

on - ly this. For - get re -
ly to - night. We must re let

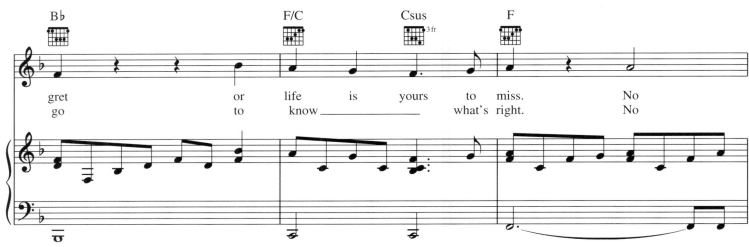

gret   or life is yours to miss.   No
go   to know _____ what's right.   No

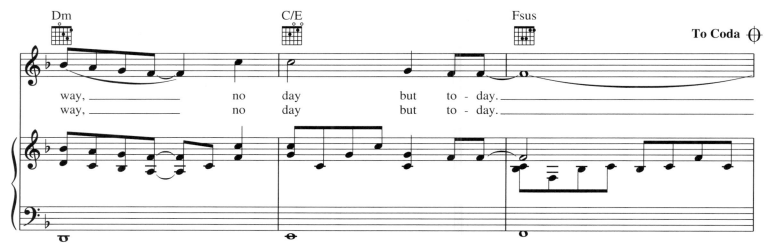

oth - er   road,   no oth - er _____
oth - er   course,   no oth - er _____

way, _____ no day but to - day. _____
way, _____ no day but to - day. _____

To Coda

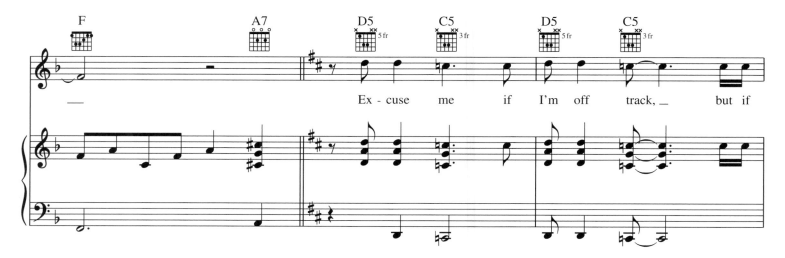

Ex - cuse me if I'm off track, _ but if

you're so wise, ___ then tell me why do you ___ need ___ smack?_

___ Take your nee - dle, take your fan - cy prayer. _

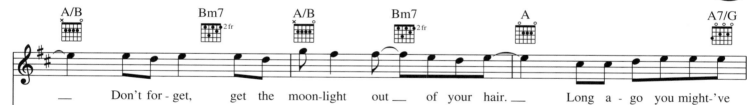

___ Don't for - get, get the moon-light out ___ of your hair. ___ Long a - go you might-'ve

lit up my heart, ___ but the fire's___ dead,___ ain't nev - er ev - er gon - na

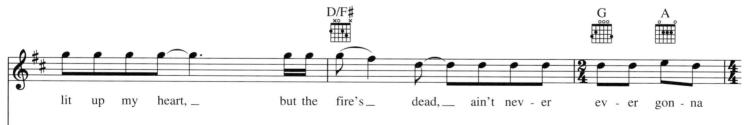

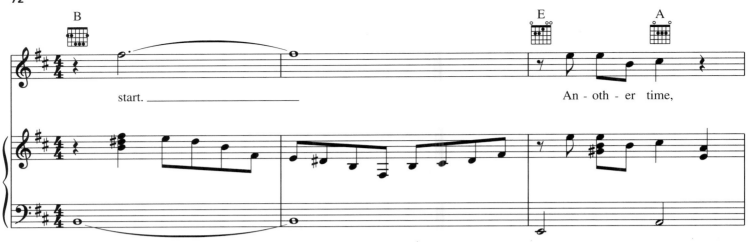

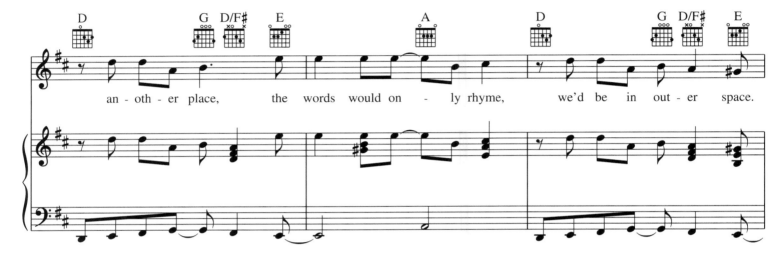

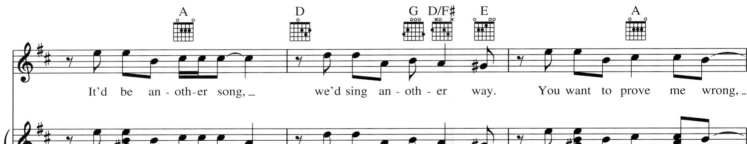

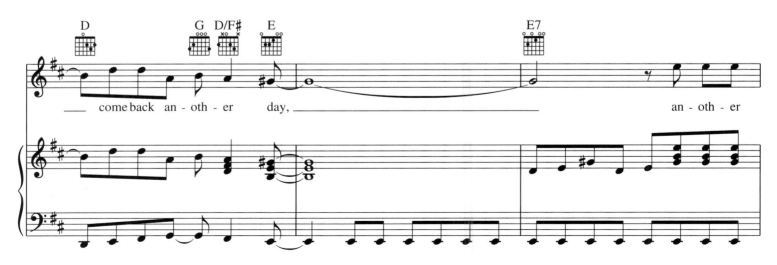

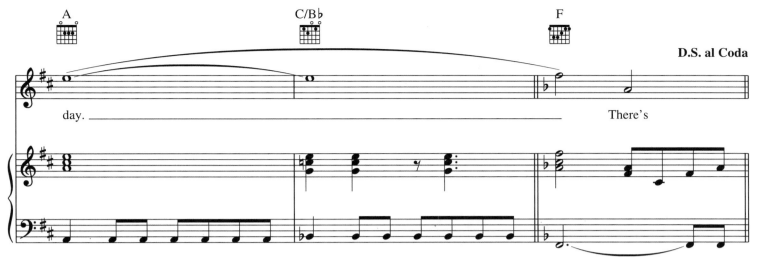

D.S. al Coda

day. _____ There's

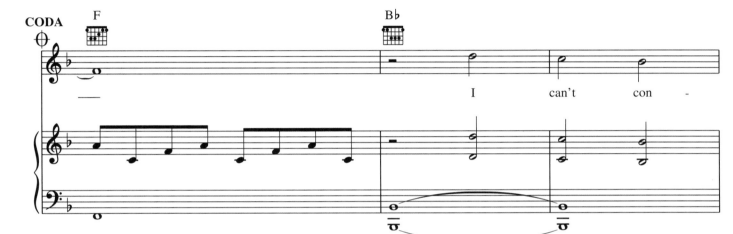

CODA

I   can't   con -

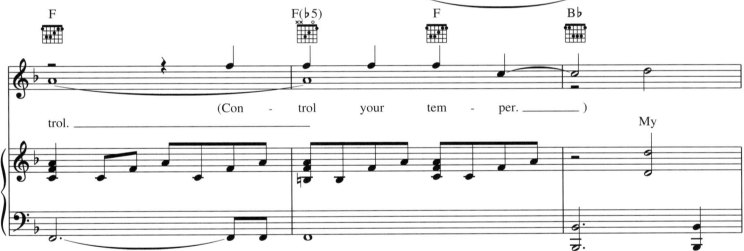

(Con - trol   your   tem - per. _____)

trol. _____   My

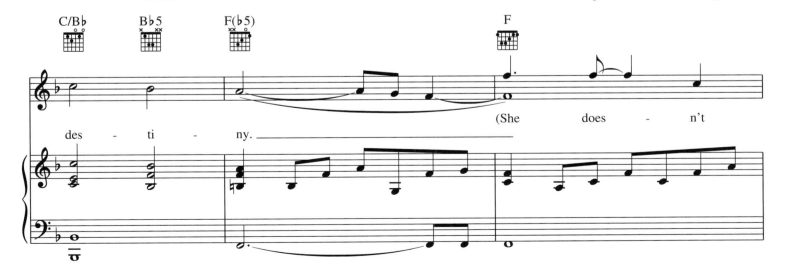

des - ti - ny. _____   (She   does - n't

WILL I?

Words and Music by
JONATHAN LARSON

Steady, not too fast

Will I lose my dig - ni - ty? __

Will some - one care? _____ Will I wake to - mor -

- row _____ from this night - mare? _____

SANTA FE

Words and Music by
JONATHAN LARSON

Moderately

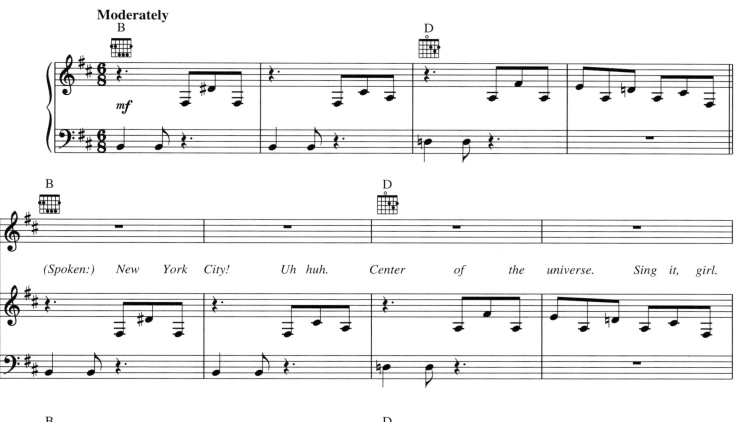

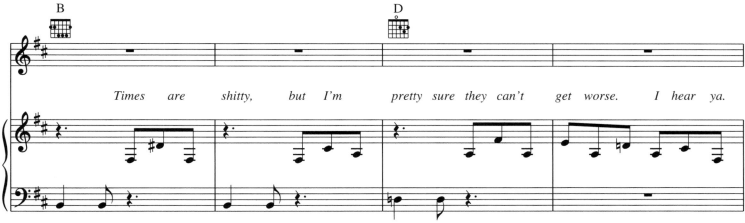

(Spoken:) New York City! Uh huh. Center of the universe. Sing it, girl.

Times are shitty, but I'm pretty sure they can't get worse. I hear ya.

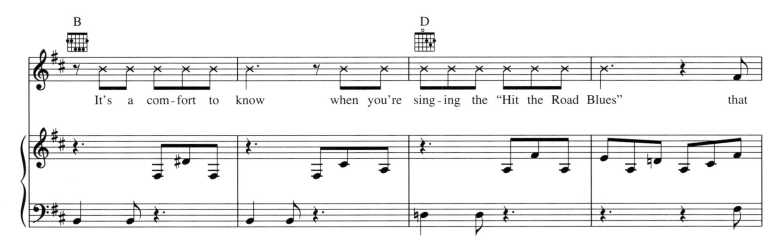

It's a com-fort to know when you're sing-ing the "Hit the Road Blues" that

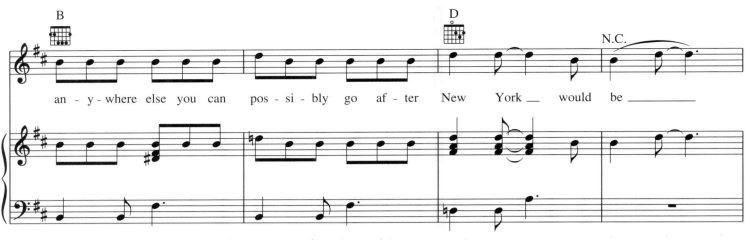

an - y - where else you can pos - si - bly go af - ter New York __ would be __

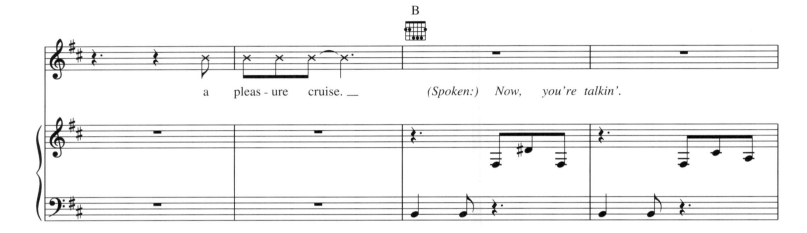

a pleas - ure cruise. __ *(Spoken:) Now, you're talkin'.*

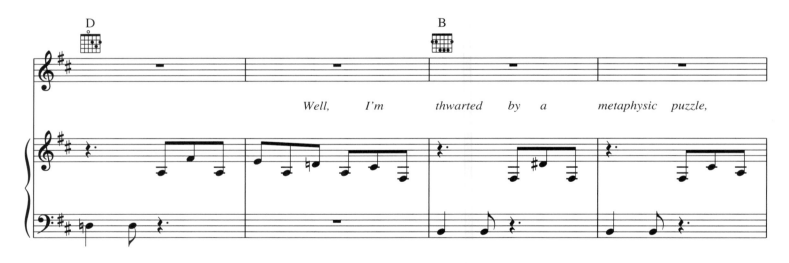

Well, I'm thwarted by a metaphysic puzzle,

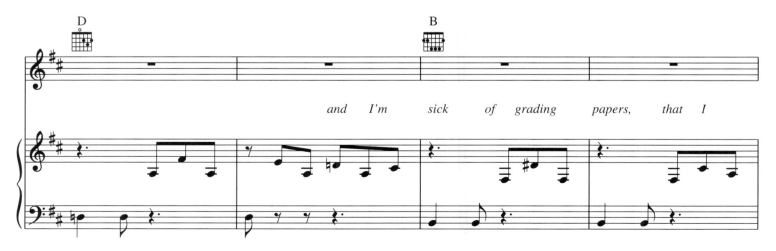

and I'm sick of grading papers, that I

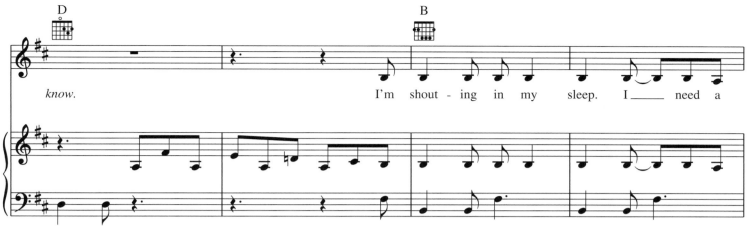

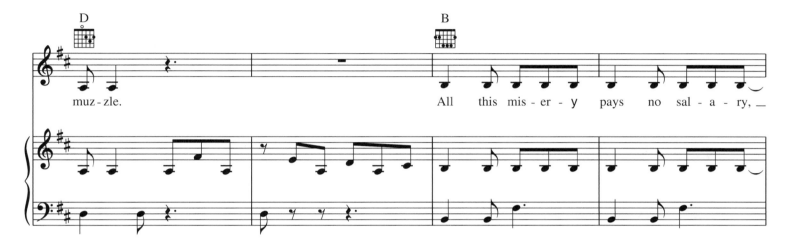

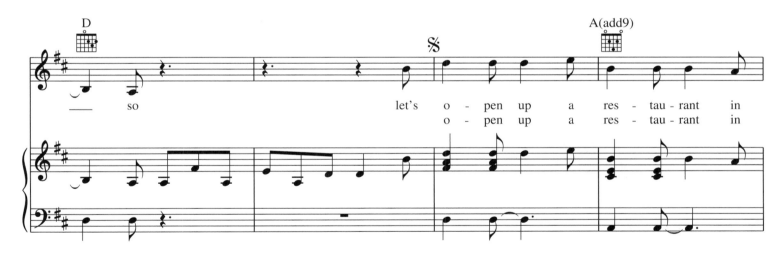

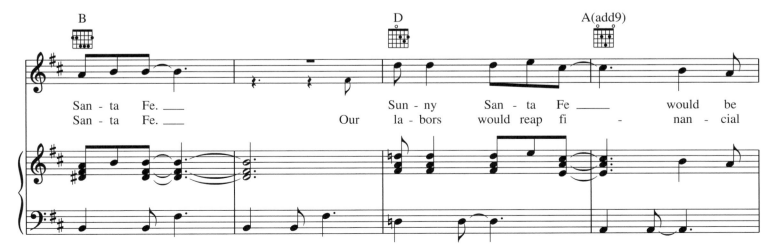

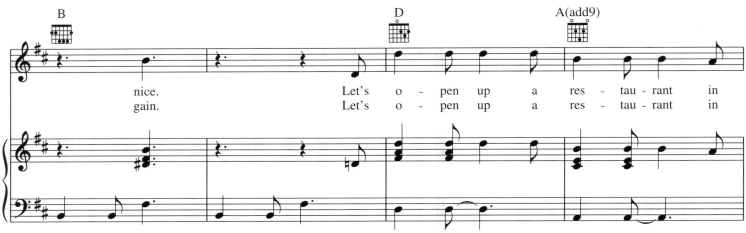

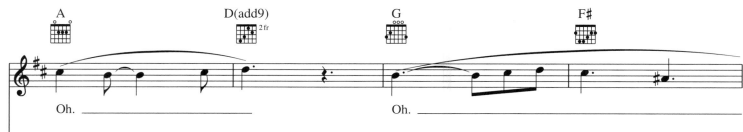

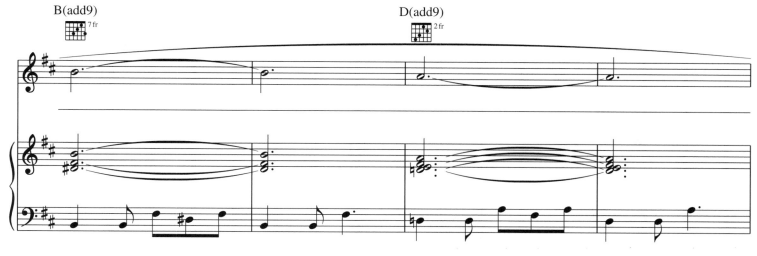

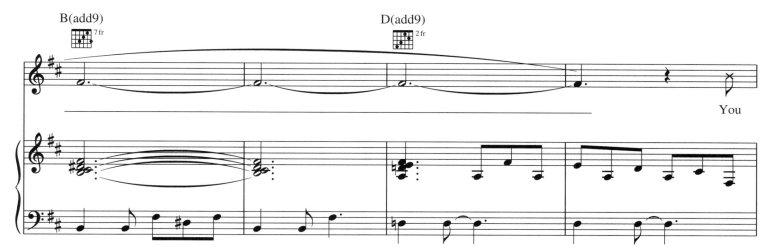

You

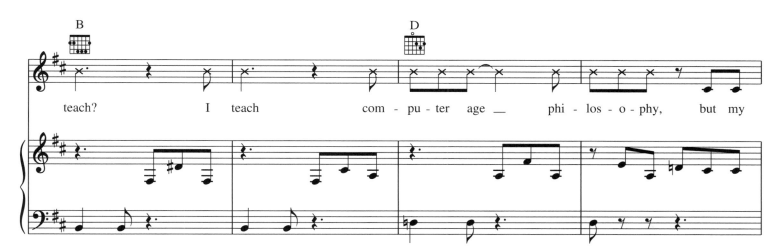

teach? I teach com - pu - ter age _ phi - los - o - phy, but my

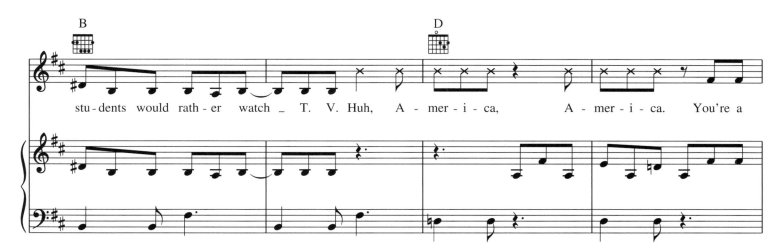

stu - dents would rath - er watch _ T. V. Huh, A - mer - i - ca, A - mer - i - ca. You're a

sen - si - tive es - thete, brush the sauce on - to the meat. You can

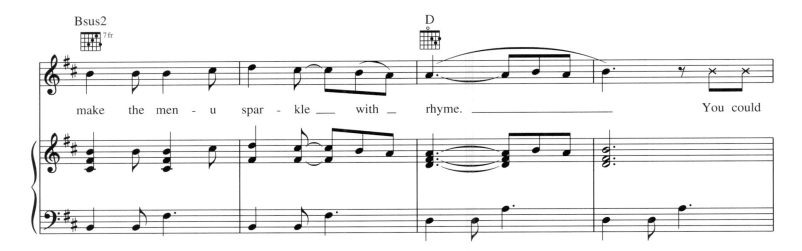

make the men - u spar - kle __ with __ rhyme. _____ You could

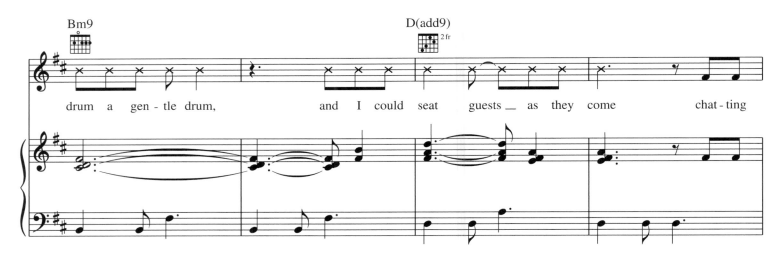

drum a gen - tle drum, and I could seat guests __ as they come chat - ting

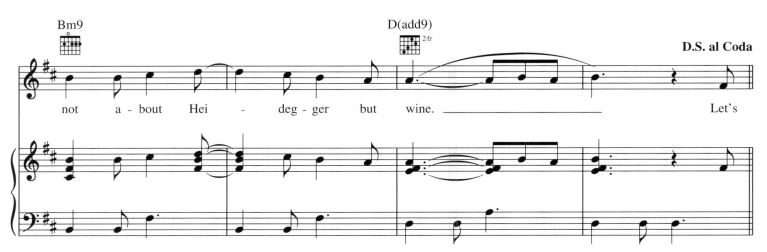

not a - bout Hei - deg - ger but wine. _____ Let's

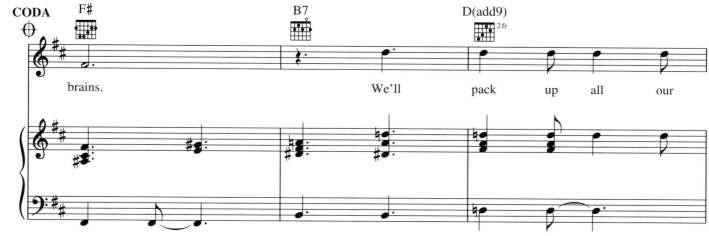

brains. We'll pack up all our

junk and fly so ___ far ___ a - way, de - vote our - selves to

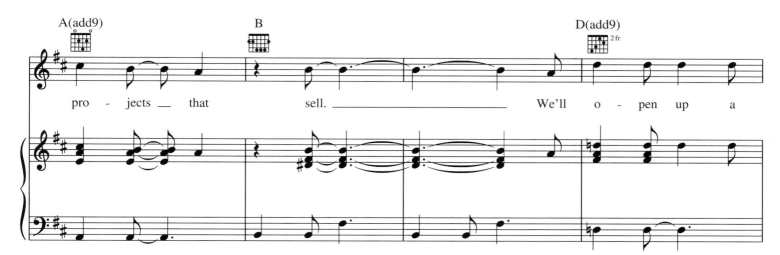

pro - jects ___ that sell. ___ We'll o - pen up a

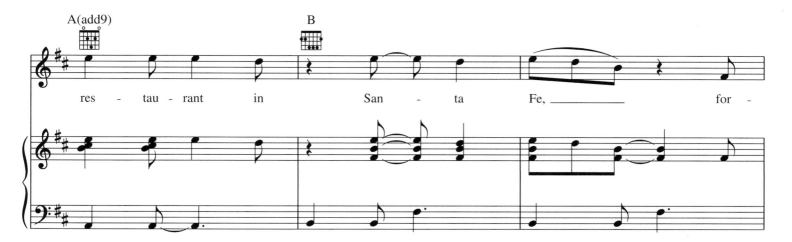

res - tau - rant in San - ta Fe, ___ for -

get this cold Bo - he - mi - an hell. _____

Oh. _____

Oh. _____

Oh. _____

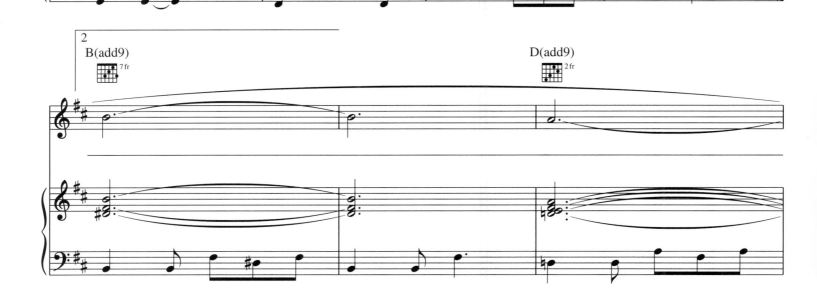

I'LL COVER YOU

Words and Music by
JONATHAN LARSON

Moderate Light Rock

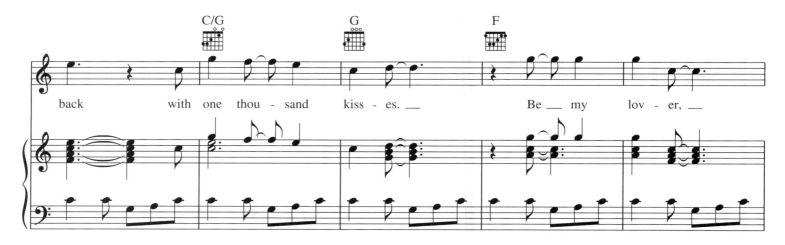

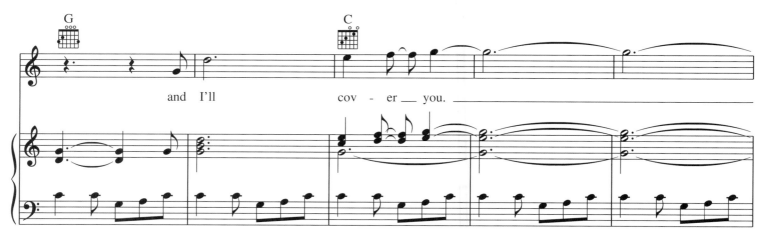

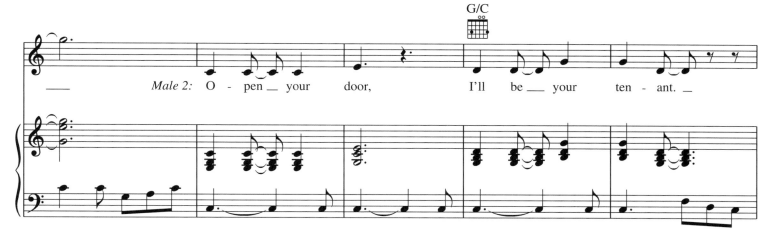

Male 2: O - pen __ your door, I'll be __ your ten - ant. __

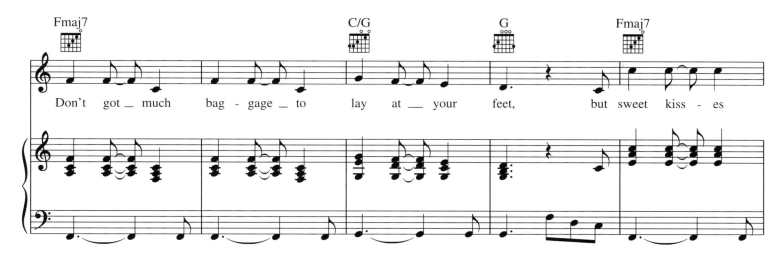

Don't got __ much bag - gage __ to lay at __ your feet, but sweet kiss - es

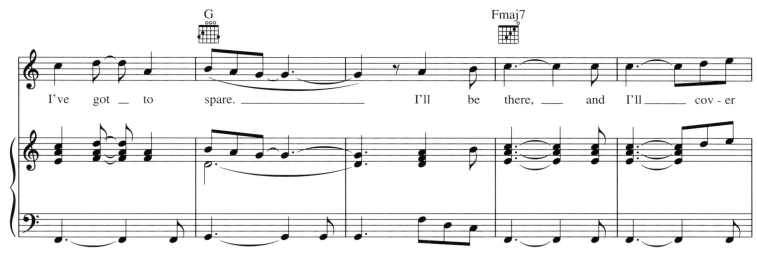

I've got __ to spare. _____ I'll be there, ___ and I'll _____ cov - er

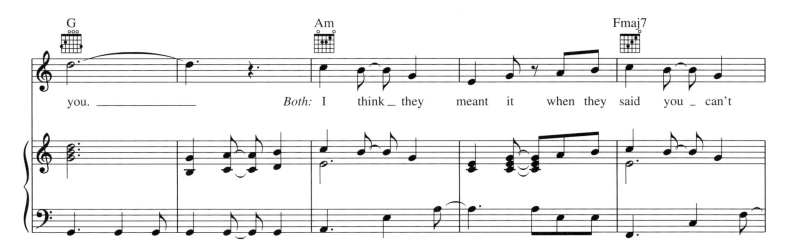

you. _____ *Both:* I think __ they meant it when they said you __ can't

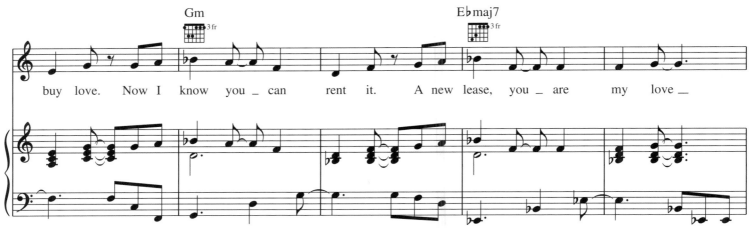

buy love. Now I know you __ can rent it. A new lease, you __ are my love __

on life. _____ Be __ my life. _____

Just slip __ me

on,   I'll   be ___ your   blan - ket. ___   Wher - ev - er,   what - ev - er,

I'll   be ___ your   coat.   *Male 1:*   You'll   be ___ my   king,   and   I'll   be ___ your

Male 2:
cas - tle. ___ No,   you'll   be ___ my   queen, ___   and   I'll   be ___ your   moat.

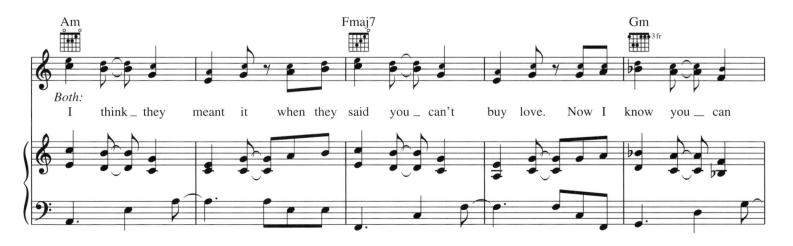

Both:
I   think ___ they   meant   it   when   they   said   you ___ can't   buy   love.   Now I   know   you ___ can

rent it. A new lease, you _ are my love _ on life, _

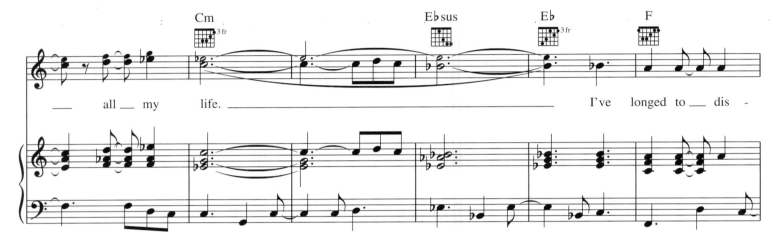

_ all _ my life. _ I've longed to _ dis -

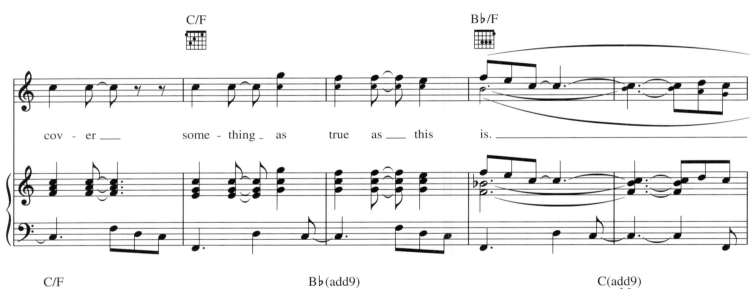

cov - er _ some - thing _ as true as _ this is. _

Male 1: If you're cold and _ you're

Male 2: So, _ with a thou - sand _ sweet kiss - es, _ I'll

Both: Oh, _____ lov - er, ___ I'll ___ cov - er you. _____

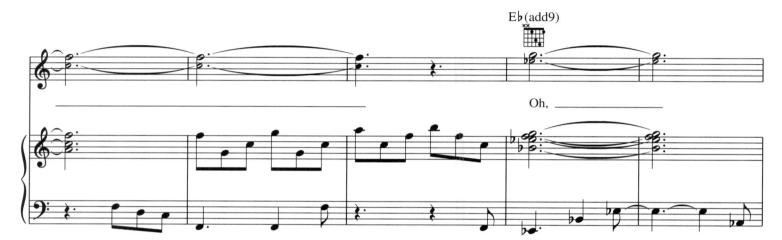

Oh, _____

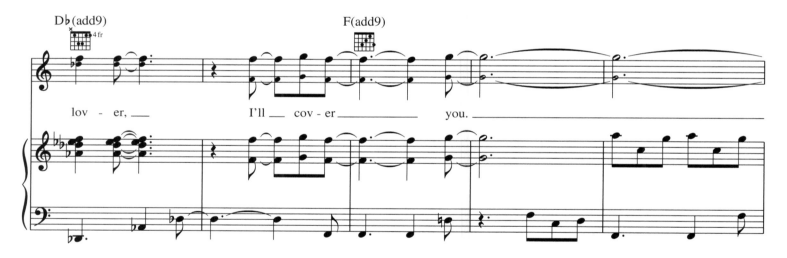

lov - er, ___ I'll ___ cov - er _____ you. _____

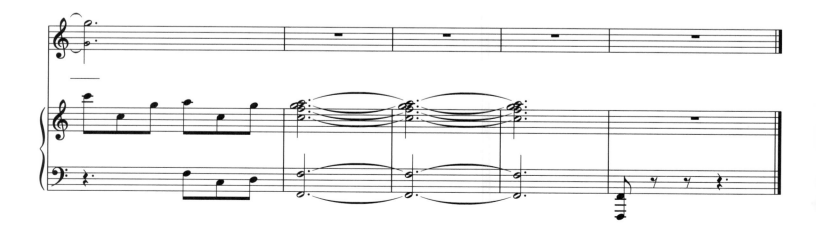

LA VIE BOHEME

Words and Music by
JONATHAN LARSON

Deliberately

Ab

Chorus: (La Vie Bo - heme.)

poco a poco accel.

mf

1

(La Vie Bo - heme.)

2

Male: To
(La Vie Bo -

Moderately fast Rock

days of in - spi - ra - tion, play - in' hook - y, mak - in' some - thin' out - ta
heme.) (La Vie Bo -

noth - in'. The need to ex - press, to com - mu - ni - cate. To
heme.)   (La Vie Bo -

go - ing a - gainst the grain,   go - ing in - sane,   go - ing mad._____
heme.)   (La Vie Bo - heme.)

_____ To lov - ing ten - sion,   no pen - sion,   to
(La Vie Bo - heme.)

more than one di - men - sion.   To starv - ing for at - ten - tion, hat - ing
(La Vie Bo - heme.)

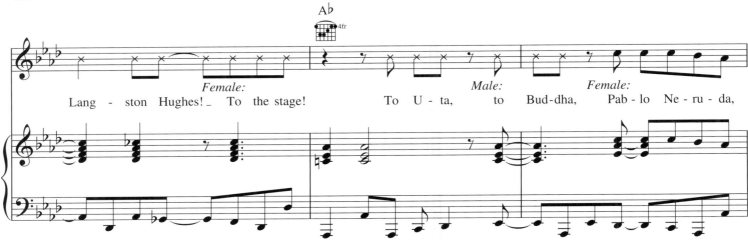

Female:
Lang - ston Hughes! To the stage!   Male: To U - ta, to Bud-dha, Female: Pab - lo Ne - ru - da,

too.   Why Doro - thy and To - to went

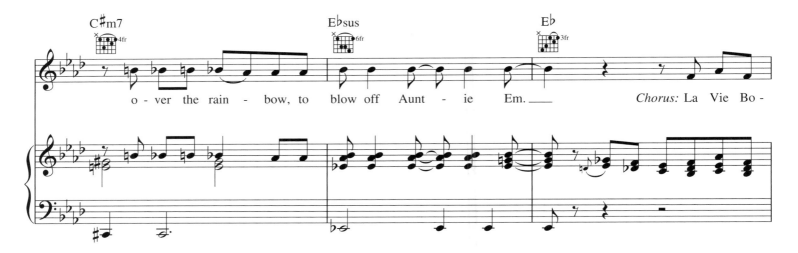

o - ver the rain - bow, to blow off Aunt - ie Em.   Chorus: La Vie Bo -

heme.

em-pa-thy, ec-sta-sy, _____ Vá-clav Ha-vel, The Sex Pis-tols, A. B.

C. To _____ no shame, _____ nev-er play-in' the fame _____ game.

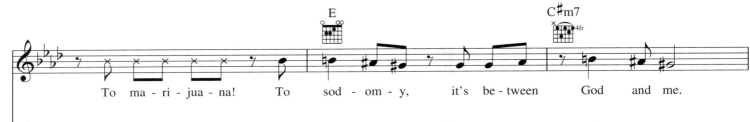

To ma-ri-jua-na! To sod-om-y, it's be-tween God and me.

To S. and M. _____ La Vie Bo-heme. _____

mon - ey, Hol - ly - wood and sleaze. Mu - sic! Food of love, e - mo - tion,

math - e - mat - ics, i - so - la - tion, rhy - thm, pow - er, feel - ing, har - mo -

ny, and heav - y com - pe - ti - tion. An - ar - chy! Rev - o - lu - tion,

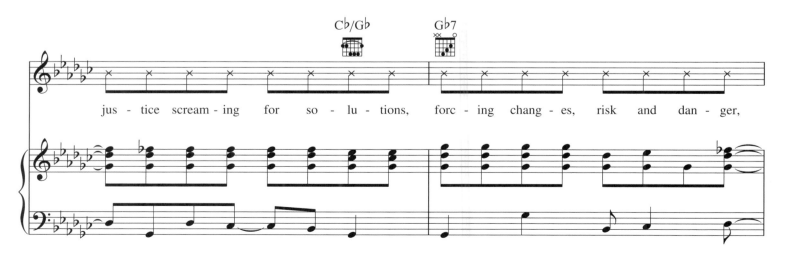

jus - tice scream - ing for so - lu - tions, forc - ing chang - es, risk and dan - ger,

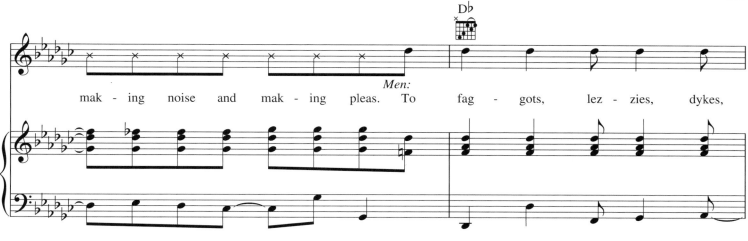

making noise and making pleas. *Men:* To fag - gots, lez - zies, dykes,

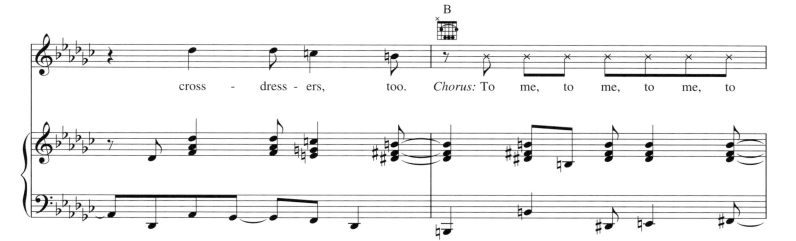

cross - dress - ers, too. *Chorus:* To me, to me, to me, to

you and you and you, you, ___ and you! *Men:* To peo - ple liv - ing

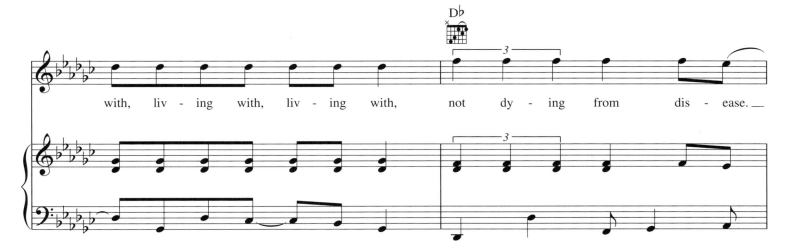

with, liv - ing with, liv - ing with, not dy - ing from dis - ease. ___

TAKE ME OR LEAVE ME

Words and Music by
JONATHAN LARSON

Ev-'ry sin - gle day ___ I walk down the street,
A ti - ger in a cage ___ can nev - er see the sun.

This I hear peo - ple say ba - by, ___ so sweet.
di - va needs her stage, ba - by. Let's have fun!

Ev - er since pu - ber - ty, ___ ev - 'ry - bod - y stares ___ at me.
You are the one I choose. ___ Folks would kill to fill ___ your shoes.

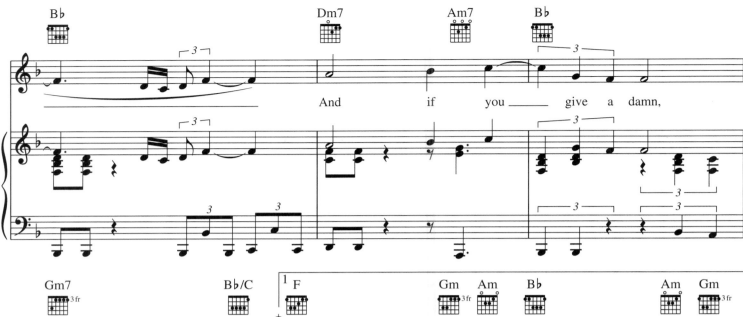

And if you _____ give a damn,

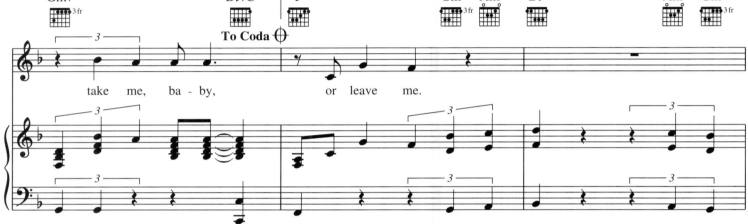

To Coda ⊕

take me, ba - by, or leave me.

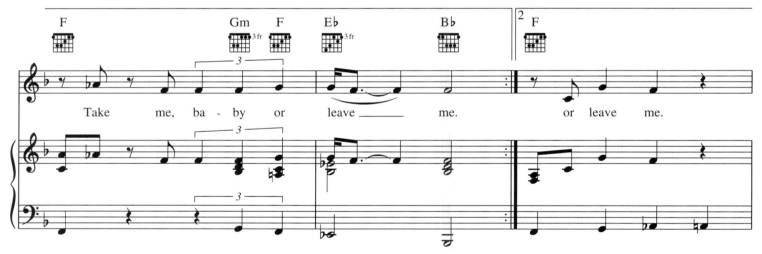

Take me, ba - by or leave _____ me. or leave me.

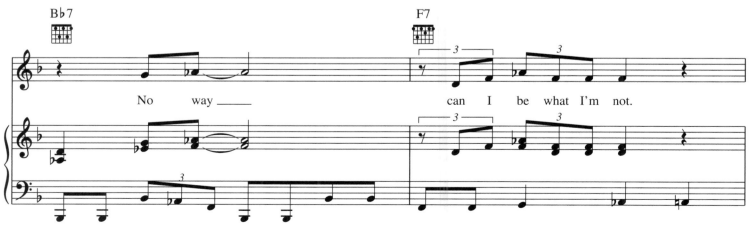

No way _____ can I be what I'm not.

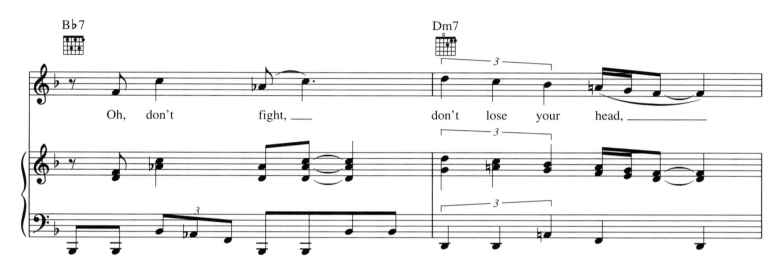

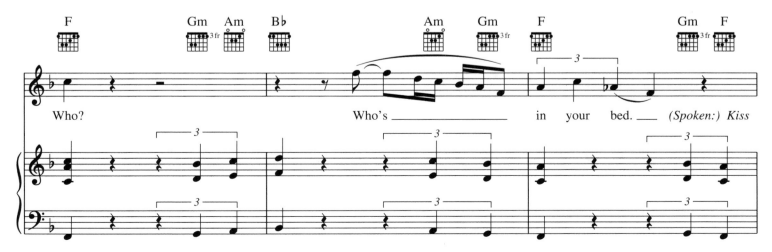

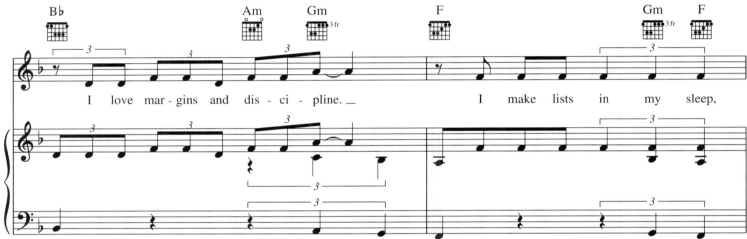

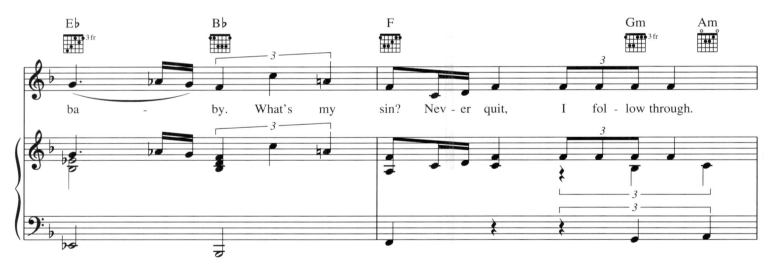

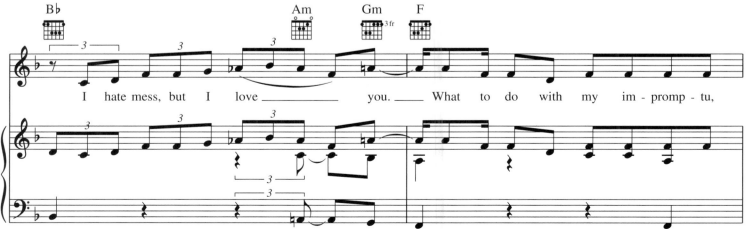

un - less you take _____ it back. Wom - en, ___ what is it a - bout them?

Can't live ___ with them or with - out them. _____

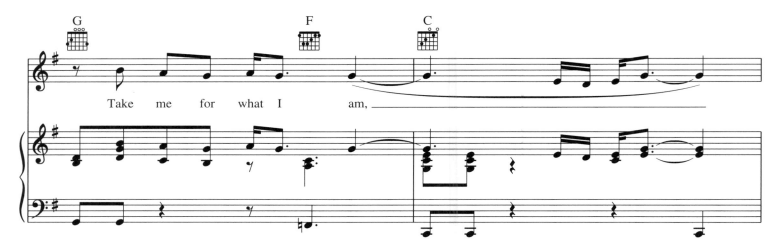

Take me for what I am, _____

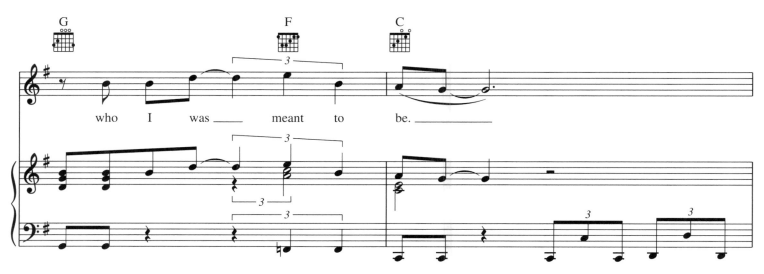

who I was ___ meant to be. _____

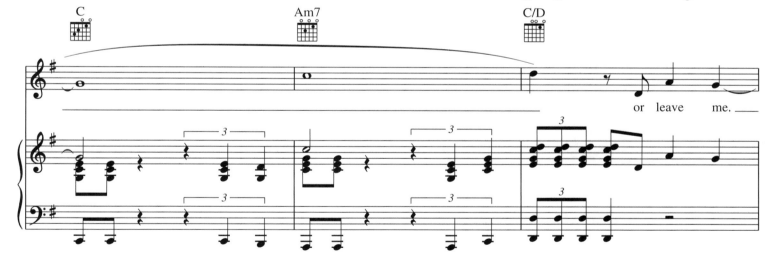

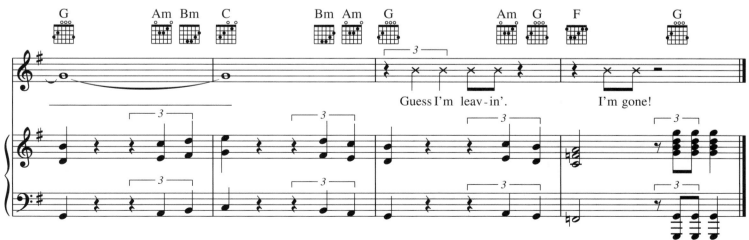

WITHOUT YOU

Words and Music by
JONATHAN LARSON

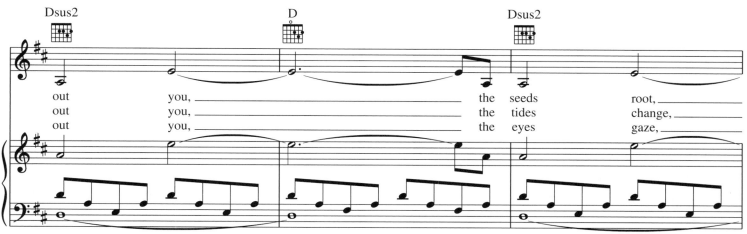

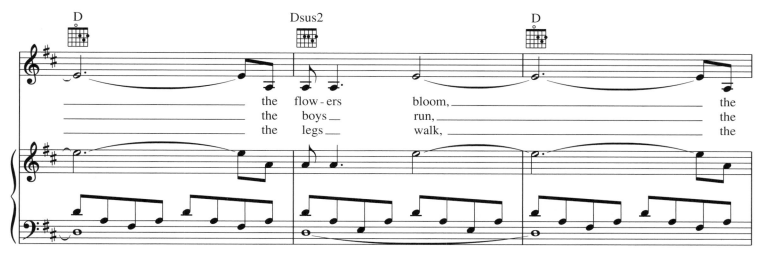

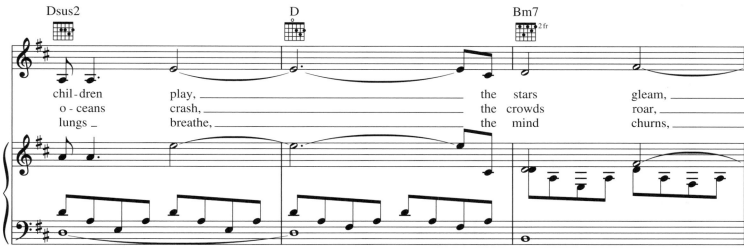

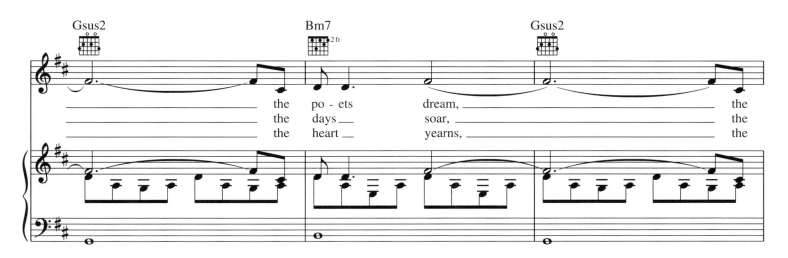

ea - gles fly _____ with - out _____ you. _____
ba - bies cry _____ with - out _____ you. _____
tears _____ dry _____ with - out _____ you. _____

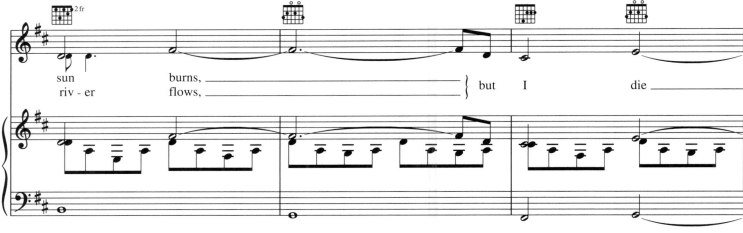

The earth turns, _____ the
The moon glows, _____ the
Life goes on, _____ but

sun burns, _____ but I die _____
riv - er flows, _____

_____ with - out _____ you. _____

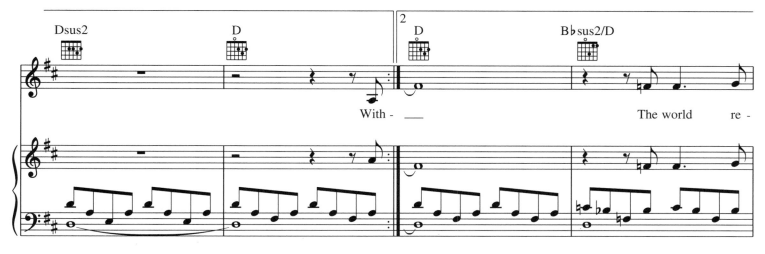

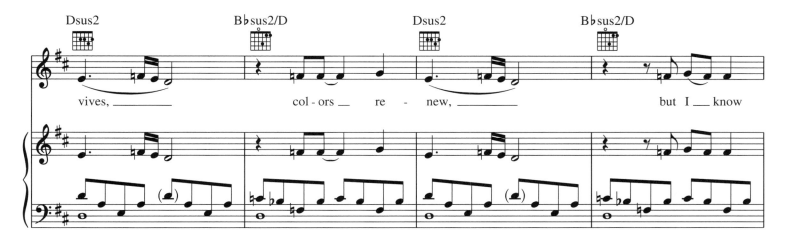

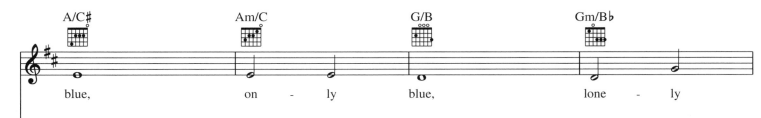

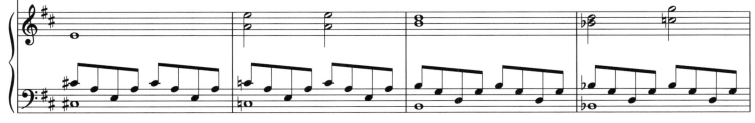

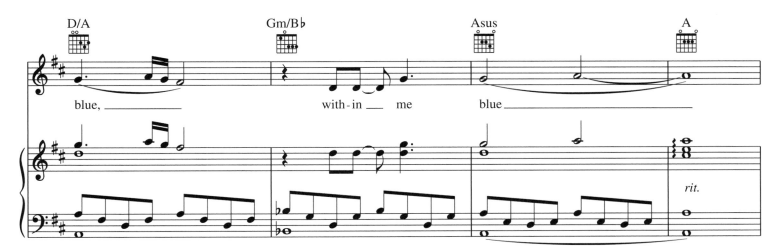

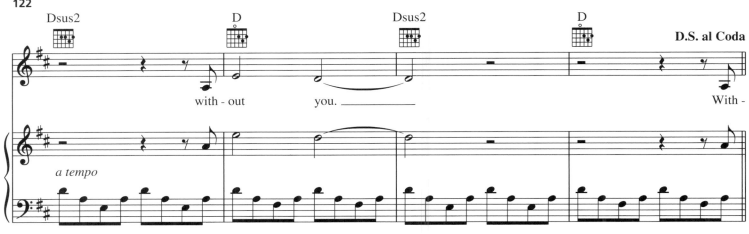

D.S. al Coda

with - out you. With -

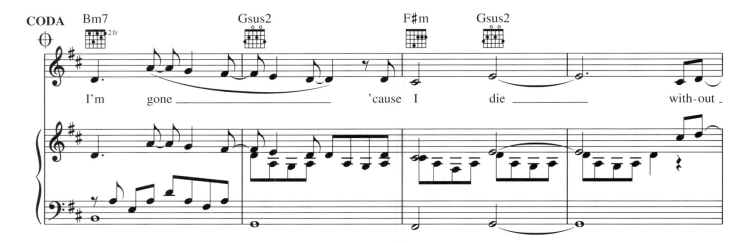

I'm gone 'cause I die with-out

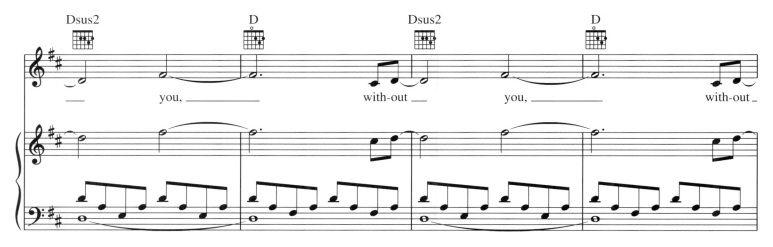

you, with-out you, with-out

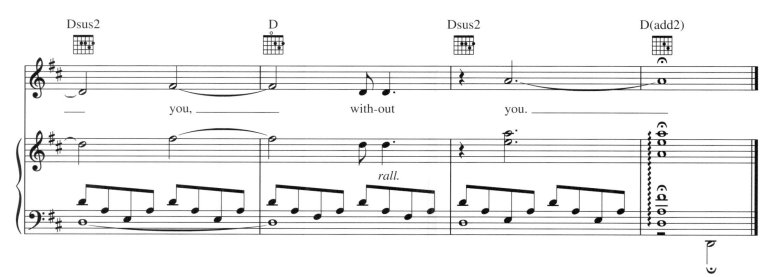

you, with-out you.

HALLOWEEN

Words and Music by
JONATHAN LARSON

Quickly

How did we get here? _

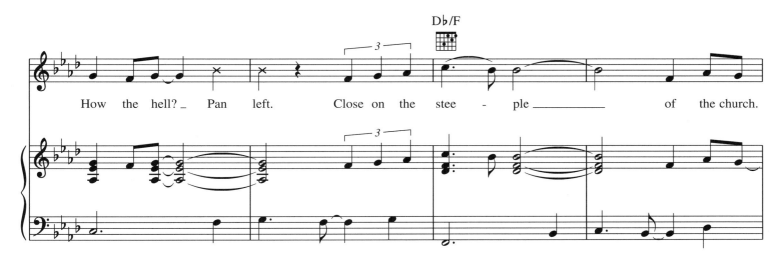

How the hell? _ Pan left. Close on the stee - ple _____ of the church.

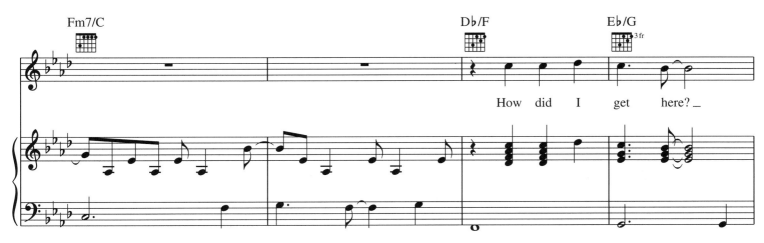

How did I get here? _

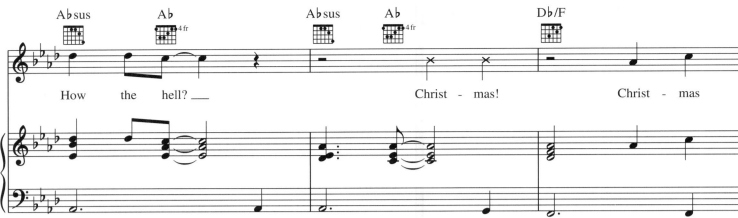

How the hell? ___ Christ - mas! Christ - mas

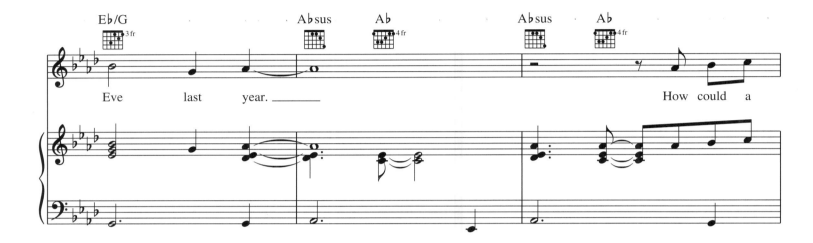

Eve last year. ___ How could a

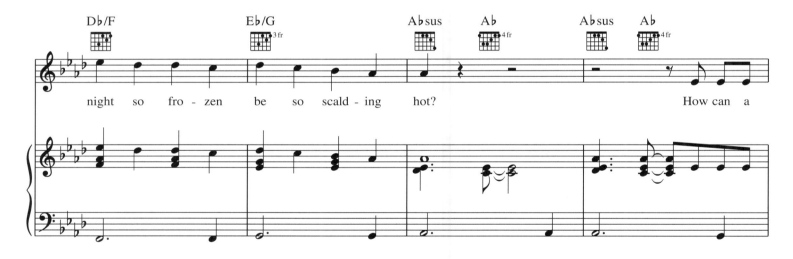

night so fro - zen be so scald - ing hot? How can a

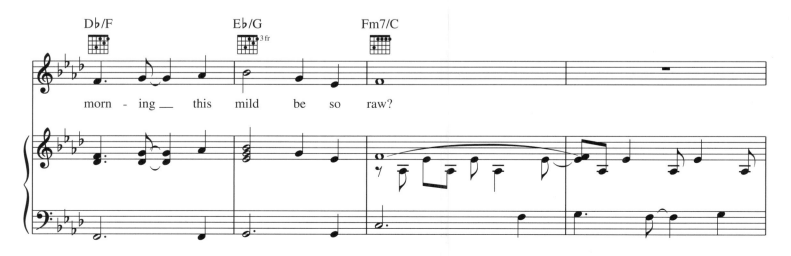

morn - ing ___ this mild be so raw?

Why are en-ti-re years strewn on the cut-ting room floor of mem-o-ry, when

sin-gle frames _ from one mag-ic night for-ev-er flick-er in close-up on the

3 - D I-max of my mind? That's po-et-ic,

Db/F   Fm7/C

that's pa-thet-ic. Why did Mi-mi knock on Ro-ger's door, _ and

Db/F   Eb/G

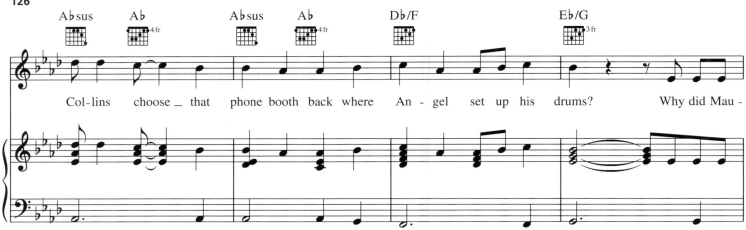

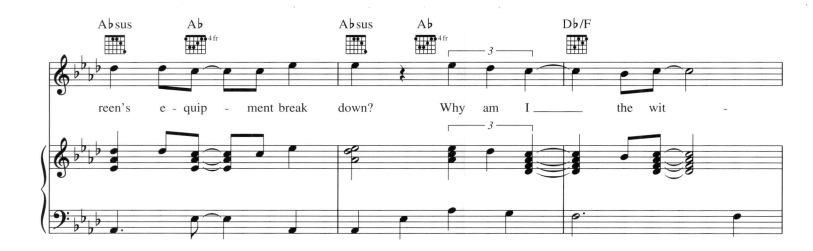

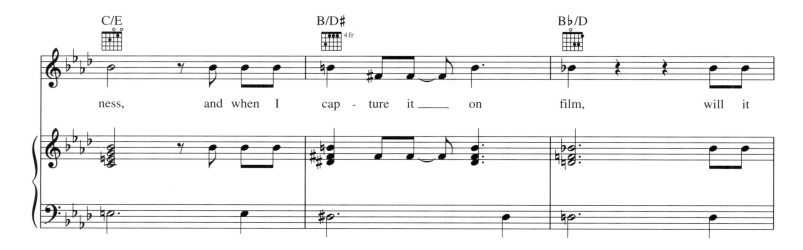

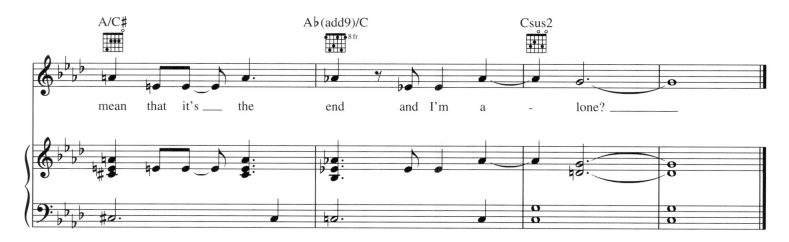

WHAT YOU OWN

Words and Music by
JONATHAN LARSON

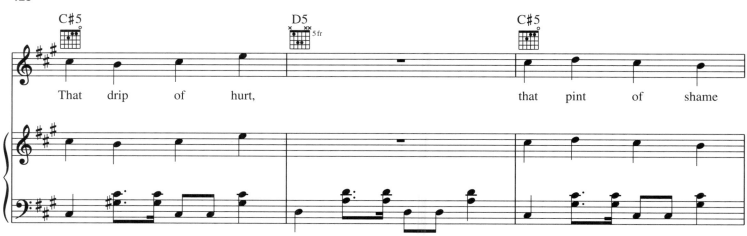

That drip of hurt, that pint of shame

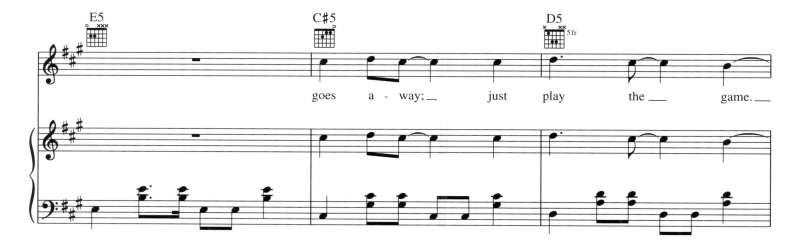

goes a - way; just play the ___ game.

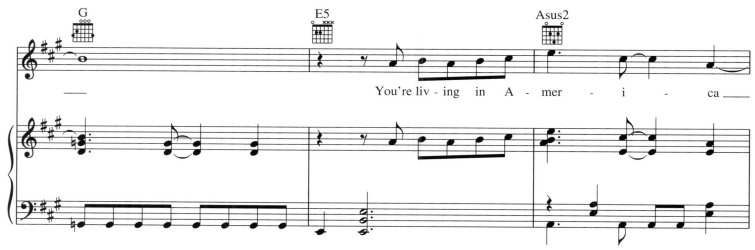

___ You're liv - ing in A - mer - i - ca ___

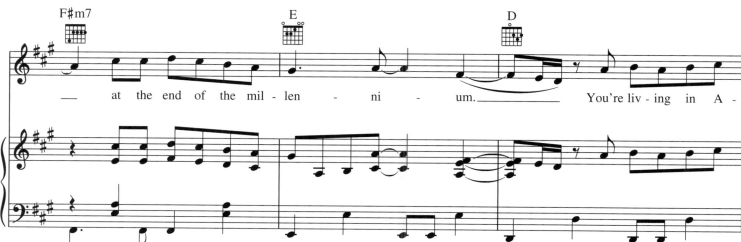

___ at the end of the mil - len - ni - um. ___ You're liv - ing in A -

film - mak - er can - not see, _____ and the song - writ - er can - not hear.

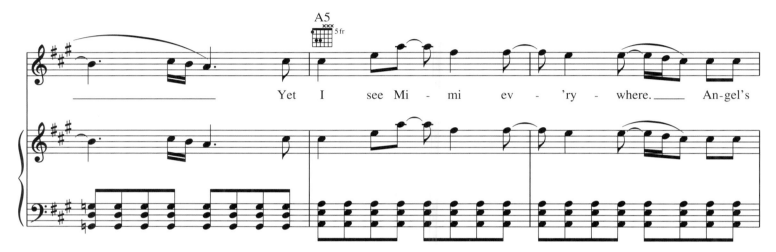

_____ Yet I see Mi - mi ev - 'ry - where.___ An - gel's

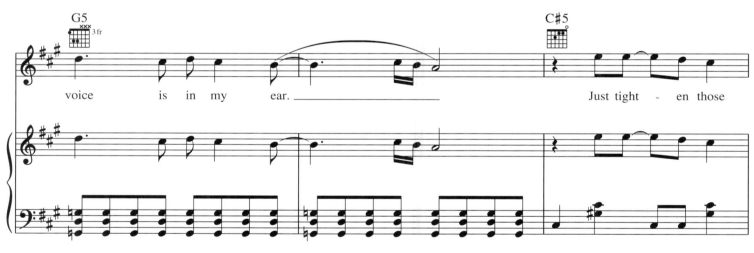

voice is in my ear. _____ Just tight - en those

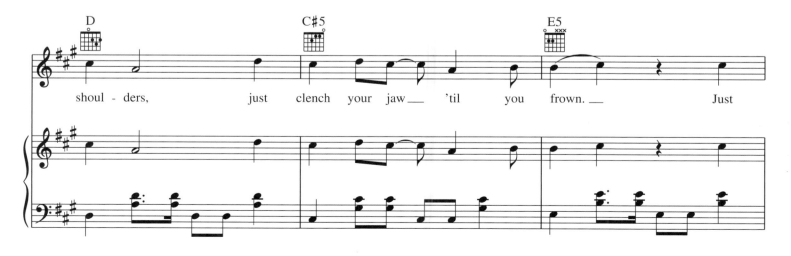

shoul - ders, just clench your jaw__ 'til you frown. __ Just

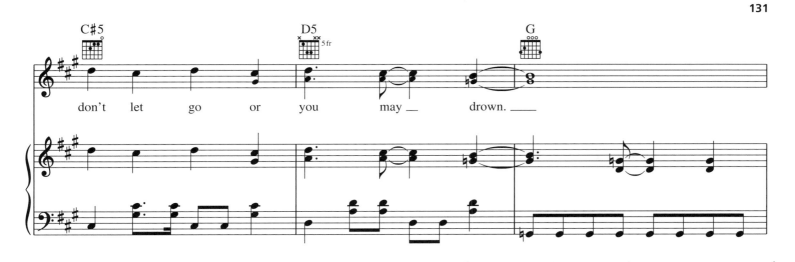

don't let go or you may __ drown. __

You're liv - ing in A - mer - i - ca at the end of the mil -

len - ni - um. __ You're liv - ing in A - mer - i - ca,

where it's like the Twi - light __ Zone. And when you're liv - ing in A -

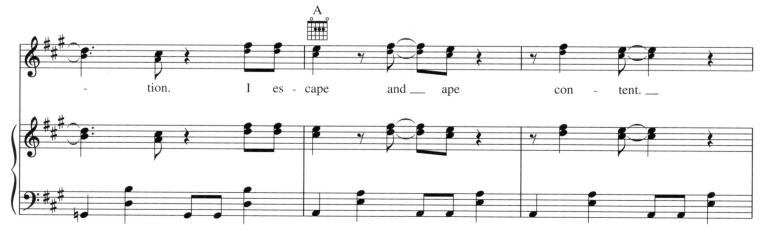

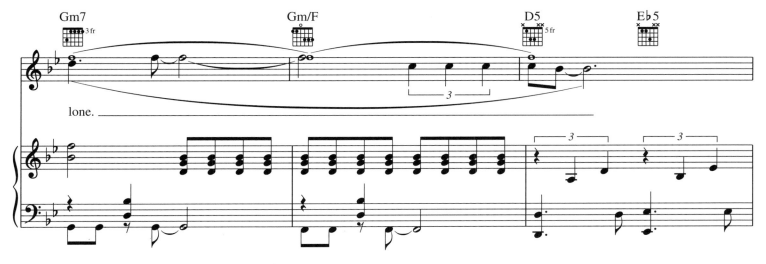

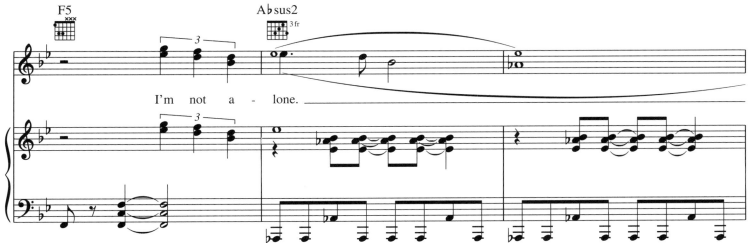

YOUR EYES

Words and Music by
JONATHAN LARSON

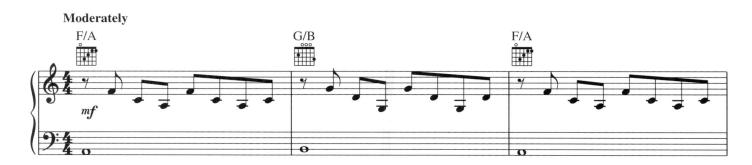

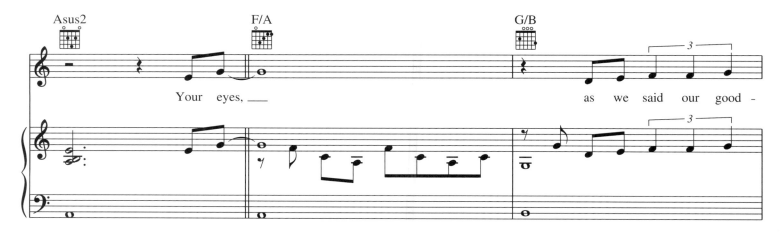

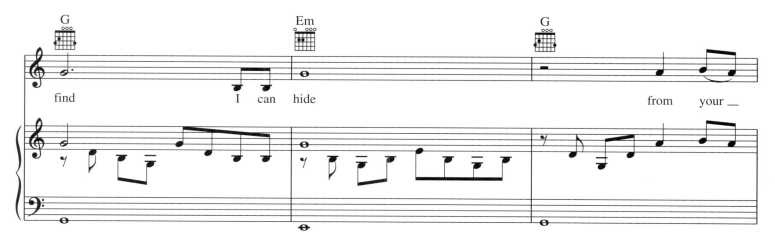

Your eyes, ___ as we said our good-byes, can't get them out of my mind. And I find I can hide from your ___

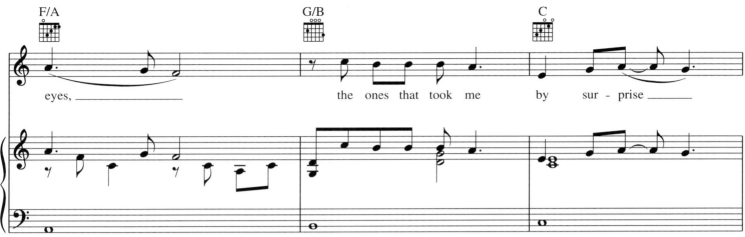

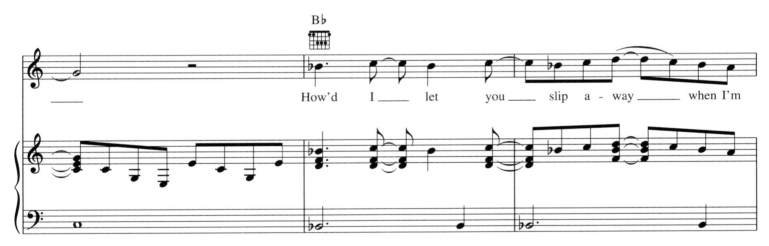

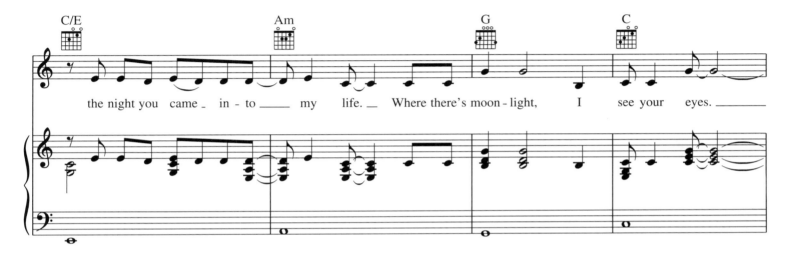

al - ways loved you. _____ You can see it in my eyes.

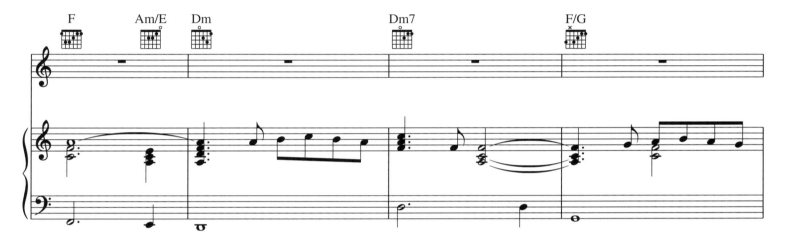

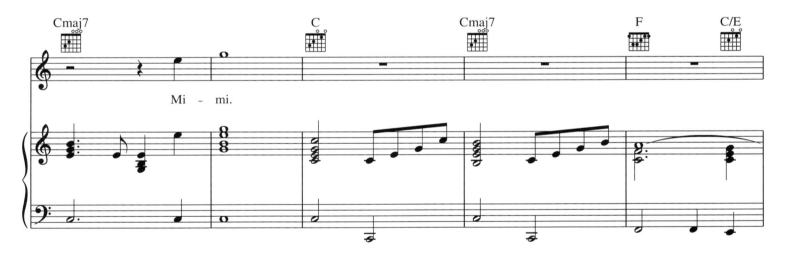

Mi - mi.

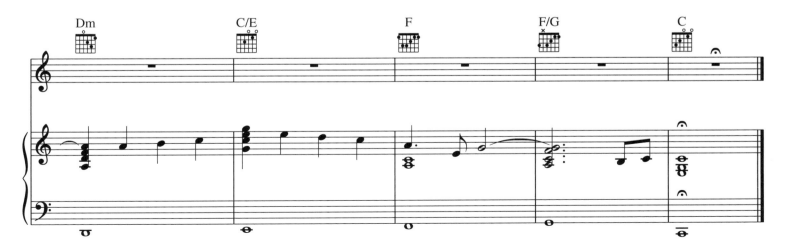

LOVE HEALS

Words and Music by
JONATHAN LARSON

walk   a - long   the   shore,   that you've walked   a thou-sand
dark,   they've lost   their   sight,   like   a   ship   with - out   a   star ___

times ___   be - fore, ___   like the o - cean's   roar, ___   *Female:* love ___

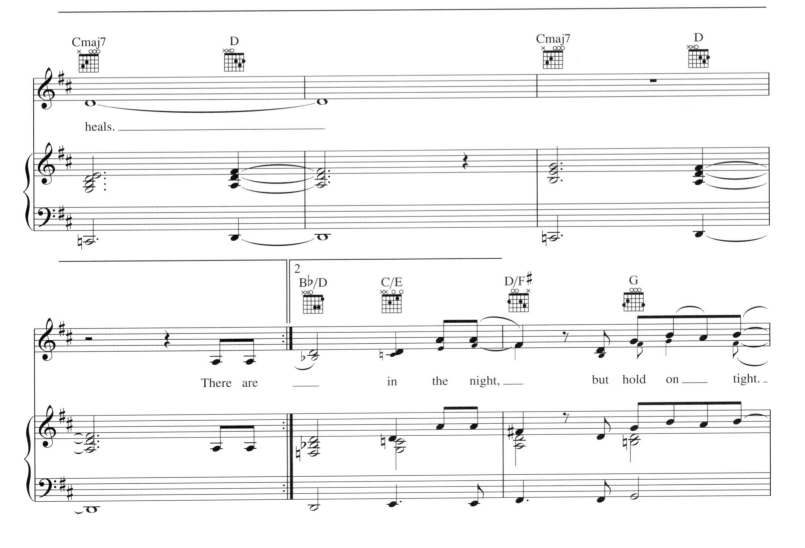

heals. _____

There are ___   in   the   night, ___   but   hold   on ___   tight. _

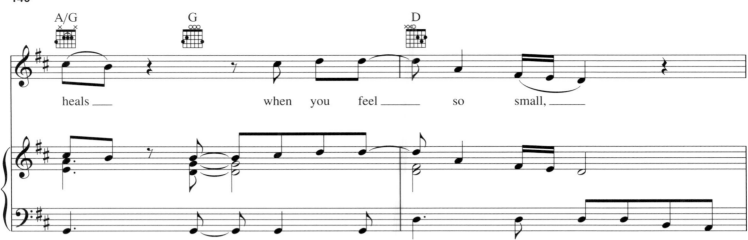

heals ___ when you feel ___ so small, ___

like a grain of sand, like noth-ing at all. ___ When you

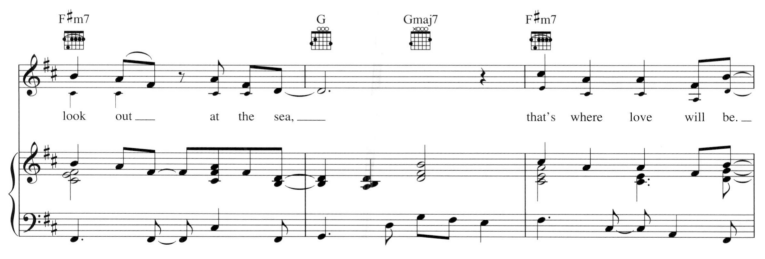

look out ___ at the sea, ___ that's where love will be. __

___ That's where you'll find me, you'll __ find me. __

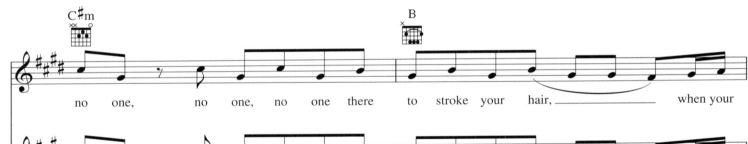

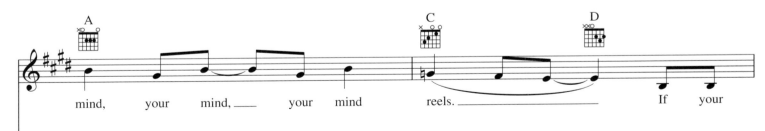

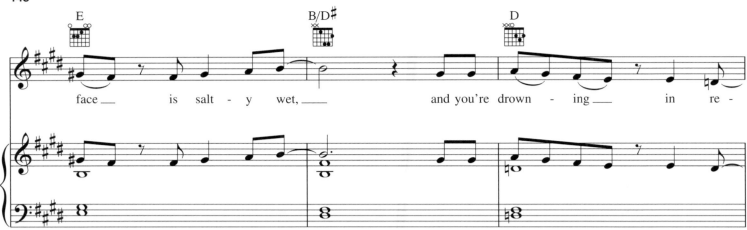

face __ is salt - y wet, __ and you're drown - ing __ in re -

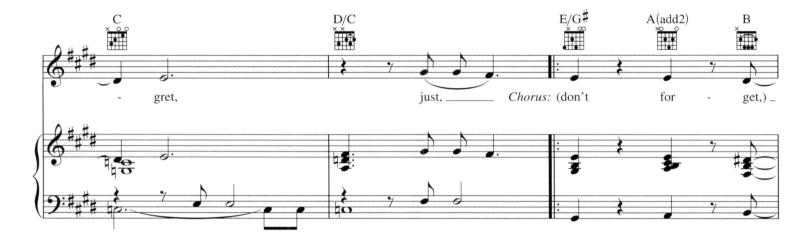

\- gret, just, _____ *Chorus:* (don't for - get,) _

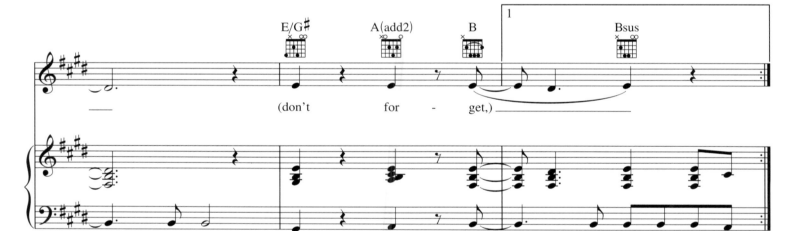

_ (don't for - get,) _____

love __ will lead you home. _____
(Don't for - get.) _

Female: Oh, keep it in your soul. _____ (Don't for - get.) _____

Keep it in your heart, _____ ba - by. _____ (Don't for - get.) _____

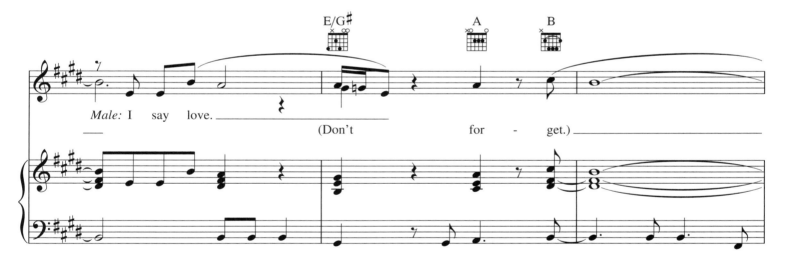

Male: I say love. _____ (Don't for - get.) _____

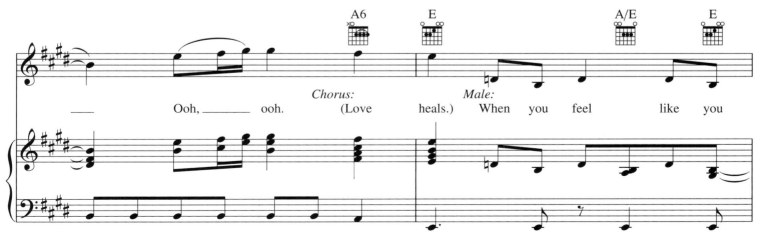

_____ Ooh, _____ ooh. (Love heals.) When you feel like you